THE ACCURSED TREASURE OF RENNES-LE-CHÂTEAU

by

GÉRARD DE SÈDE

In collaboration with

Sophie de Sède

Translated into English

by

W.T. Kersey

and

R.W. Kersey

To the memory of Abbé Joseph Courtauly

DEK Publishing

THE ACCURSED TREASURE OF
RENNES-LE-CHÂTEAU

Le Trésor Maudit de Rennes-le-Château

By Gérard and Sophie de Sède

English translation by W.T. Kersey and R.W. Kersey

Website by Shane D. O'Brien of Cumorah Hill Publishing

Copies of this book available from the publisher's website:

www.greatdiscoveries.co.uk

Postal requests to:

DEK Publishing

57 Farm Way, Worcester Park, Surrey. KT4 8SB

E-mail: dekpublish@lineone.net

Printed and bound in England

by Ebenezer Baylis, Worcester

Typeset in Perpetua 15 pt

2nd Edition

Copyright © Editions Julliard, Paris, 1967.

First published as

L'OR DE RENNES OU LA VIE INSOLITE DE BÉRENGER SAUNIÈRE, CURÉ DE RENNES LE CHÂTEAU

English Translation Copyright © DEK Publishing, 2001.

Cover design by Shane D. O'Brien.

Cover - The château and village of Rennes, 2001. Sepia by Bill Kersey

A CIP catalogue record for this book is available from the British Library

Publisher: DEK Publishing, a subsidiary of DEK International Limited

ISBN 0-9541527-0-0

TABLE OF CONTENTS

LE TRÉSOR MAUDIT DE RENNES-LE-CHÂTEAU

The original copyright holder of the J'ai Lu series edition in 1967 was René Julliard who was approached in 1973 when the translation was first undertaken. Though the rights for the English translation were available, publication did not proceed at the time, but a private copy was made available to the BBC in support of their productions.

The translation has now been revised in 2001. Illustrations have been maintained as first published apart from minor cosmetic changes to improve the clarity of the site plans and diagrams. A sketch map of the area has been included. This work stands as reference material for those who would make a serious study of the subject.

ACKNOWLEDGEMENTS

We particularly wish to recognise the technical publishing advice from John Windell and especially the tireless work of Shane and Lydie O'Brien of Cumorah Hill Publishing. We are grateful for the support received from Béatrix Vernet of Robert Laffont S.A.

Gérard de Sède has stated that researches of the type necessary to achieve the particular requirements of this book are always difficult and they cannot result in a successful conclusion without the involvement of numerous participants. He particularly wished to recognise the work of Colonel Arnaud, Director of Communication Personnel for the Army; M. René Chésa; M. Corbu; M. Jacques Debant, Director of Departmental Archives for Aude; M. René Descadeillas, Keeper of the Library of Carcassonne; Commandant Edmond Lerville, President of l'Association des Réservistes du Chiffre; Doctor Malacan; Count Maraval de Niort; Abbé Maurice-René Mazières; de Sède's colleague Pierre Pons, of the *Dépêche du Midi;* M. Vilcoq, cryptographer, together with contributions from those persons who have desired to remain anonymous, which contributions were nonetheless most precious.

<u>BACK COVER (1967)</u>

As the nineteenth century drew to a close, was the tiny village of Rennes-le-Château, set on a hilltop in the Aude the centre of a fabulous discovery beyond our wildest dreams? What was the secret possessed by Abbé Bérenger Saunière who, between 1891 and 1917, disposed of more than one and a half thousand million of old francs valued in 1913 at sixty million pounds? But, how can anyone explain why all who would take this matter lightly — as much now as in the past — could so easily be putting their life in jeopardy?

To all these questions, Gérard de Sède takes great pains to address those issues with precision and objectivity. Thus the enigma of Rennes-le-Château, with all the violent deaths that are linked to it, is not something that one may confront without risk. Nevertheless, this impassioned and courageous study allows the student a deep insight into this fantastic tale of hidden treasure.

ooOOoo

There is a certain similarity existing between the facts that have been reported in this book and an imaginary construction. However, this is the result of pure chance. But it is not in the least surprising, because the similarity is certainly remarkable.

Gérard de Sède, 1967.

FOREWORD

The publishers of the original French version of *LE TRÉSOR MAUDIT DE RENNES-LE-CHÂTEAU* by Gérard and Sophie de Sède, have kindly agreed to the publication of this translation into English.

This book will be welcomed by all those who have followed the progress of this saga throughout the years. Many and varied are the theories that have been expounded to give meaning to the strange events that have unfolded amongst the rugged mountains of the Razès. Perhaps with a new millennium, now is the time to return to the basic facts, as far as they may be determined. The first translation was undertaken in 1973 when the tale was young and the trail was relatively fresh.

I know that this book will fill a niche that has long been empty. Many will share the pleasure that I have gained in its preparation. We may all find a treasure in its spoken word. There are those who still cherish the recollection of the original French text. They will enjoy this book as much as those who see it for the first time. Those who have trodden the devious paths of Rennes will savour the excitement felt by Gérard de Sède as he set out on his journey of discovery.

Perhaps we may share in the feelings and thoughts of Marie Denarnaud as we shoulder a portion of the burden carried by Abbé Bérenger Saunière who once held a secret in his hand and kept it too well.

Bill Kersey, London 2001.

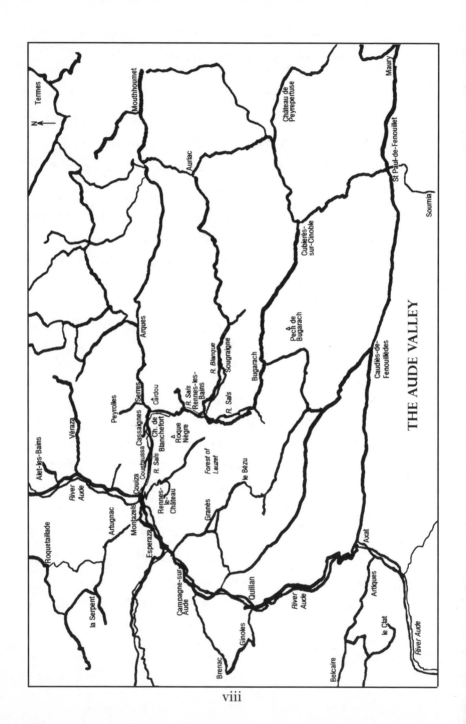

THE AUDE VALLEY

PART ONE

THE DEVIL IN HOLY WATER

When the traveller, having passed Carcassonne, continues his journey up the valley of the Aude, he all too soon leaves the fertile countryside for a wild wasteland riven with gullies. This is surely a land that both nature and history have striven to torment: the Razès. A blue sky and red ochre terrain, violently contrasting, seem to illustrate the perpetual quarrel of Heraclitus and Zeno, the contest between turbulent chaos and stagnant order.

The ilex oaks, the gorse, rock roses, lavender and thyme cling with the energy of despair to the tawny rocks, which are pierced with numberless caves as if torn by giant teeth. Here and there may be seen the ruins of a castle, the indestructible witness of ages that yield up their secrets with reluctance. At Limoux one should not fail to sample the sparkling local wine, as further on it will be too late;

the Razès is richer in water than in wine. It is not only a land of springs, but is also a land rich in metals. Nature has heavily impregnated the streams with minerals and their waters are of an intolerable bitterness, which serves only to increase one's thirst. But if one does as did the queens of long ago and bathes therein, then they possess the mysterious power of healing.

We first pass the Benedictine Abbey of St Hilaire, whose cloister is curiously decorated with a chequer board carved in stone, then we reach Alet, the ancient site of the temple of Diana, which town Pope John XXII designated a bishopric some six centuries ago (though today it has fallen from its high estate). We then come to a sunken road, flanked on the left by the peak of Cardou and on the right by the unstained rock of Blanchefort backed by the sombre rampart of Roco Negro as the road continues up towards Rennes-les-Bains.

This thermal spa is today rather unimposing, though it was well known to our more distant ancestors, and in fact was the centre of social brilliance at the time of the Roman conquest. In this village, where a statue of Isis has been unearthed, are to be found three thermal springs, known respectively as the Queen's Bath, the Strong Bath and the Sweet Bath. Nearby there are two cold springs; the Ring, which is rich in iron, and the Magdalene, or the Gode, where the Blanque and Sals rivers converge at a place called Le Bénitier. Here the water eddies over a slab of green stone, seeming to adorn it with crystal florets.

Coming from the mountains, these springs usually only

emerge after a long subterranean passage, often through a series of siphons that serve to regulate their outflow. In a country where dry summers after the spring thaw can greatly vary the water table, the remarkable reliability of these springs gave rise to a holy veneration, so that White Ladies and Black Virgins disputed the superiority of one spring over the other. So in ancient times in Arcadia did the Alpheus River suddenly disappear beneath the ground only to reappear in Sicily as the sacred spring of Arethusa.

This mythological parallel attracted the attention of a nineteenth century author, Labouisse-Rochefort, whose journey to Rennes-les-Bains opens with this somewhat insipid line:

"From thy happy Alpheus, O thou dear Arethusa..."

Surrounding this little town of the waters, the mountains provide a beautiful reddish crown, interspersed with a white and green patchwork as pastureland, rocks and forests alternate. Here one may distinguish the remains of a vast megalithic enclosure. To the north-west was to be found a menhir, known as Cap de l'Hom, The Man's Head, because it was decorated with a carving in relief of a human face. Removed at the end of the nineteenth century, this strange sculpture is now situated at Rennes-les-Bains, in the presbytery garden: some say that it bears the face of the Saviour, others that it is the head of Saint Dagobert.

Eastwards there spreads a vast tableland, the plateau of Lauzet. Here can be found the Pla de la Coste, where two huge stones, some tons in weight, the Rollers, may be rocked on their pedestal when the least force is applied. Lower down, there flows the Dead Man's Brook. To the east, the platform of a dolmen is found next to the entrance to a jet mine, and a curious pile of rock bears the name of the Bread Stone since a large round block rests upon a flagstone, like a loaf of bread upon a table. On this flagstone there are five deep cups, resembling the imprint of five fingers and known as the Devil's Hand. In these parts the devil has certainly greatly enriched local toponomy. Here there is his breast, and there his armchair.

Finally southwards, towards the Serbaïrou, one may observe a raised stone in the shape of a geometrically perfect gaming die.

It all forms a phantasmagoric landscape where it is difficult to distinguish the art of early man from the fantastic vagaries of nature and which tempts the observer to do his archaeology by pure guesswork.

At one time Rennes-les-Bains was merely the Baths of Rennes, the spa suburb of another Rennes, the ancient Aereda, later known as Redae or Rhedae, from which Rhedesium and later the region of Razès drew its name. This town, with a population of some thirty thousand, once dominated the plateau that surrounds it. It was powerfully fortified, and according to the poet Theodulphe, "Inde revidentes te, Carcassonna Rhedasque…", was on a par with Carcassonne. The later Visigoth kings in the sixth century selected it as one of their two capitals, the other being Toledo which was razed to the ground in 1361 by the terrible

Aragon mercenaries of Henri de Trastamare. Today nothing remains except a village that has been ravaged by successive fires and is found on the map with some difficulty. This is Rennes-le-Château.

As the crow flies, the distance between the two Rennes hardly exceeds three kilometres. But unless you sprout wings, the route is long and winding, even dangerous. The murmuring of insects and the scents of the moorland make the road more suitable for a gentle ramble as it leads you up to Rennes-le-Château. Rising above the surrounding countryside, like a piece in a game of chess, the village provides a vantage point from which the vistas across the valleys of the Aude and the Sals present panoramas of equal beauty.

On one side, the view embraces the small market towns of Campagne, Laval-Dieu and Bézu, where the Templars held three commanderies. On the other side can be seen Arques and the ruins, lofty and fire-charred, of Coustaussa, which as its name indicates is the custodian and watchful guardian of these wild regions.

The expired Rennes-le-Château still retains its castle and its châtelain. With its fine lower hall of the Visigothic era such as is rarely seen today, its Renaissance façade and its tower, the mansion, which formerly belonged to the illustrious families of Voisins and d'Hautpoul is picturesque but completely dilapidated. The old man who lives there now (and somehow survives) will display to you, should you manage to persuade him, the fruits of his strange labours. He has accumulated a collection of stones in capricious shapes in which he claims to discern the fossils of men and of animals once alive in some Atlantis and later cast up from the sea. He may also show you the atlas of maps. These he has built up over the years so that the whole of France is by his agile brush populated with mythological people, whose exploits and achievements are revealed, according to his system, in the names of now unimportant villages.

Before the door of the castle there flourishes an age-old mulberry[1] tree, whose fruits like hearts streaming with blood, give to those who would gather them, red stigmata upon their hands.

A hundred paces from here upon a terrace open to the wide horizon, is arranged an assemblage of monuments of almost aggressive luxury, in the taste insisted upon during the nineteenth century, and of an ugliness which could soon cause one to forget their special significance. There is first a two storey Neogothic tower, square, castellated, on which one may read with surprise the word "Magdala". One corner of the tower is flanked by a circular watch-tower. Next, there is a walkway of semicircular form, which is supported by a succession of rooms and leads to a spacious orangery topped by a conical glass roof. This whole assembly encloses a fair sized park adorned by a formal pond and by precisely aligned pathways.

---

1. The mulberry was introduced into France by Pope Clement V. (Bertrand de Goth). In Languedoc it is named *Amourié* and in Spain *Moral*. According to fable, it was under this tree that Pyramus and Thisbe died through their love.

Finally one arrives at the once-comfortable villa of the former inhabitant and it will be noted that a carving of the Sacré-Coeur surmounts the door while on the façade is engraved the word "Bethany".

Close at hand there is the ancient village church, much patched since the eleventh[1] century. Because of its simplicity, at any rate when viewed from the outside, it presents us with a contrast. For hardly have we entered when we are overcome by a disturbing uneasiness. The first thing we encounter is a misshapen devil that supports the holy water stoup. And then, by degrees, our eyes will discern a whole population of statues of aged men who look like caricatures frozen into unusual postures, all clothed in their varied colours and fixing on the visitor their unnerving glassy stares. It's Saint-Sulpice gone mad, a Grevin Museum of the scriptures. But soon, in spite of oneself, one has to linger in order to re-examine this strange world where every detail seems to have been arranged, one knows not to what design.

The builder of all this? Some of those who knew him are still living. We have interviewed them one by one. By degrees, the records have been laid bare; it is thus that we have uncovered the prodigious story of the Abbé Saunière.

ooOOoo

---

1. This church was consecrated in 1059 to St Madeleine.

François Bérenger Saunière was a child of the country, born in the Aude at Montazels on 11th April 1852. The house where he was born may be seen to this day. In front of it stands an imposing fountain, with wrought iron surrounds, where the water gushes from its beautiful dolphins that were sculpted in the eighteenth[1] century. Despite their modest conditions, his parents cared well for their seven children. François was the eldest one, and for the eldest special efforts must be made. Without doubt, this is what enabled him to follow an ecclesistical career. Ordained in 1879, he first became Curate at Alet and then Parish Priest of the humble village of Le Clat. Perhaps he foresaw a brilliant career when he was promoted after three years to be professor at the seminary of Narbonne. But he did not remain there longer than a month; being intelligent and headstrong, he had too much independence of spirit and his manners were too self-assured to meet with the approval of his superiors. On 1st June 1885 they therefore appointed him Parish Priest of Rennes-le-Château, though they did not guess that they had opened up to him whom they had exiled, the doorway to a fateful destiny completely without precedent.

At the age of thirty-three, a significant age for a Priest, Bérenger Saunière has ended his life as a man without a history. He does not delay in his restoration to life in the character of the hero of a fabulous adventure.

If one attempts to reawaken the memory of their pastor among his one-time parishioners, who are now

---

1. Jean-Bernard Carles built this fountain in 1751.

bowed with age, they will all exclaim:

"Ah he was a fine man!" and their eyes will suddenly light up. Photographs show him to us as being large of stature, square and broad-shouldered, as if ready to charge. The plebeian countenance is not without a certain brutality, which seems to be accentuated by the carnivorous jaw; but this is offset by the wide lofty forehead crowned with close-set hair. The eyebrows are heavy, the eyes black, beautiful and alive, the gaze penetrating, restless and disturbing. The energetic chin smoothes down to a dimple, which if one is to believe the popular fancy, is the never-failing sign of the tempter.

To such a man, Rennes-le-Château serves only as a prison. The village contained only some two hundred inhabitants. It was poor, far away from anywhere, almost out of this world. It could only be reached by a rough road, barely fit for mules. The church of St Madeleine was falling into ruins, and through its leaky roof the raindrops were free to fall from Heaven upon the officiating Priest. The presbytery had become quite unfit for habitation so that the new Priest was forced to seek lodgings with one of his flock, Alexandrine Marro, a grasping old dame who extracted from him a high rent.

At that time, the State still held responsibility for the payment of Priests, but Saunière, classed as a militant reactionary by reason of an ill-timed pre-electoral outburst, soon found himself deprived of his rightful stipend. Then he was faced not only with poverty, but also with misery and black despair.

Through the lack of ability to pay his rent, he was compelled to install himself in a dilapidated and tumble-down cottage. Looking through his account-books for this period, we note the following entry:

"Amount due per month to Alexandrine Marro —Year 1890 July–August: food and bread, 25 francs." For sixteen months he spent in all only 90 francs expenses and 25 francs for rent. And there is this mention revealing a cynical sense of humour,

"Secret funds: 80 francs 25 centimes."

Being athletic the Priest satisfied his thirst for exercise with fishing and hunting: for him the little streams yielded their agile trout while over the moorland slopes his gun often bagged a red-legged partridge, which local folk commonly term the "rare game". This was no mere sport for it often served to augment the poor fellow's meagre meal.

His thirst for knowledge was no less than his physical energy: he read extensively and would have read even more if his pocket had been less shallow. He perfected his Latin, and learned some Greek and even attempted Hebrew. He delved into the rich history of the Razès region and studied the families who had held lands thereabouts and the derelict capital city into which a thankless destiny had cast him.

He also visited an older neighbour, Abbé Boudet, the Parish Priest of Rennes-les-Bains, a learned man, and the author of some curious works.

There remained the appetites of a man in the prime of life. Marie Denarnaud, a maker of hats and some eighteen years old, quitted her place of work in order to become his rather unconventional maidservant. It was said that she was of a jealous nature and therefore fastened sprays of gorse to the windows of the presbytery, since their golden flowers are commonly held to serve as a protection against witchcraft. In all this, there seems to be little that is abnormal. However, more uncommon, also more mysterious, is the solidarity they displayed in the face of every ordeal, the indestructible complicity that, even up to the final day, served to unite these two so dissimilar human beings. Even on the occasions of his triumphs and of his flattering conquests, Bérenger did not dream for a moment of separation from Marie; while Marie, though crushed by old age and beset on all sides, never surrendered the secret which she had shared with Bérenger.

If he suffered by reason of his own poverty, Saunière regretted still more the destitute condition of his little church. By a lucky chance, one of his predecessors, Abbé Pons, had bequeathed to the parish the sum of six hundred francs. In 1888, thanks to this small legacy, our Curé found it possible to carry out the most urgent repairs. Then, after much pleading, he at last persuaded the unwilling municipality to allocate to him a far more substantial loan, amounting to fourteen hundred francs.

Without any clear ideas as to when or how he was to settle such a debt, towards the end of 1891 he ventured to proceed with the work.

The high altar was the most beautiful ornament in the church. It rested upon two antique columns of the

Visigothic era, on which crosses and hieroglyphic symbols were finely carved. But the stone table was in a most decrepit condition. It spoiled the overall appearance and needed replacement.

Saunière undertook the task, helped by two masons, Rousset and Babou. The heavy flagstone was first removed, and it was noted with surprise that one of the pillars was hollow, and stuffed with dried ferns. In this nest of leaves, there rested three wooden tubes sealed with wax: when opened, they were found to contain parchments.

Since this discovery had been made in the presence of witnesses, it was soon common knowledge.

"Let us preserve these ancient documents with the other communal archives." proposed the mayor, whose mind was fettered by red tape. But Abbé Saunière had other views and declared that the parchments would only go mouldy if deposited in the mayor's office and would therefore benefit no one.

"Now there are in the large cities, many enthusiasts in the field of antiquities who would surely give a good price for such documents. It would be better to sell them. I could take care of that."

The astute Curé had touched a tender spot, since to the villagers money was always welcome. It was therefore decided that Saunière should endeavour to sell the documents, on condition that he should draw from the proceeds an amount at least equal to the loan that had been made to him for the repair of the church. In this way, nothing would be lost.

Finally however, since the peasant sense of mistrust was strong, the mayor insisted that he be given exact tracings of the documents that he could preserve. Certainly only the Curé was capable of carrying out such a task of laborious scholarship. We have actually handled two of these tracings, and will discuss them again in due course.

It was at the start of 1893 that Abbé Saunière decided to show his discovery to the bishop. The Bishop of Carcassonne was then Félix-Arsène Billard, a wise and farseeing man, who possessed many important connections. He examined with great care the four parchments submitted to him.

The conversation between the two men was reported to us as follows:

"Did you really consider disposing of these documents?"

"To tell the truth, Monseigneur, I really had no such intention. But they are difficult to decipher. For over a year now, I have struggled with them for many nights without success. I have therefore come to seek your advice."

"You must go to Paris." replied the prelate. "I am acquainted with ecclesiastics who are very familiar with palaeography. Here is a letter of introduction."

"To Paris? But, Monseigneur, I do not possess even the first sou for the journey."

"That is of no consequence, the diocese will certainly pay for the cost of your journey."

"I have never left the Aude, Monseigneur. In Paris I shall be afraid of getting lost."

"That surprises me very much, my son, since you do not lack either energy or assurance. Also you will find many reliable guides there."

"Monseigneur, there is one other matter. The mayor is well aware that these documents are to be sold to repay the money lent to me; if I don't succeed in selling them, what shall I do upon my return?"

"Do you believe that the bishopric of Carcassonne is so impoverished that it cannot find fourteen hundred francs? You will be quit of this matter, as it is only a white lie. I give you my absolution in advance."

Thus did the penniless little country Priest leave for the capital. Once settled in the train that was to carry him to Paris, we can imagine him like a second Rastignac dreaming of the wickedness of the Ville-Lumière. And in fact, it turned out to be a truly surprising expedition.

As soon as he arrived, Bérenger Saunière proceeded to Abbé Bieil, the director of Saint-Sulpice. When he had read the bishop's note, he welcomed our hero, and then carefully examined the four unintelligible scribbles; after which he asked his visitor to entrust them to him for a week, the time necessary for their submission to the specialists.

What is one to do in Paris when one has little money? Saunière knew hardly anything about the place. By chance Bieil introduced him to his nephew, Ané, an editor of religious publications, who offered him bed and board. He also introduced him to his grandnephew, Émile Hoffet.

This young lay brother had hardly yet found his feet, but at the age of twenty he already spoke several languages, was interested in the Middle Ages and had also studied palaeography and cryptography under the learned Abbé Baguès. He was then only at the commencement of a lengthy career of research that was to lead him on several missions to the Vatican and would cause him to dedicate his studies to the field of occult arts and secret societies.

Through these various members of his host's family, the country Priest came to realise how unjust is the reputation for lack of taste that has been attached to the church that was built by Olier, the visionary Abbé of Pibrac. In truth there is nothing commonplace about Saint-Sulpice, the "New Temple of Solomon".

Saunière was suitably impressed by the sight of the Stations of the Cross as set out in the reverse direction, by the astronomic dial, by the inscriptions, now alas defaced, which indicate in the transept the Paris meridian, and by the three beautiful holy water basins. He duly admired the pictures bearing the signature of Delacroix, and the unusual crucifixion by Signola. He also read the plaque that commemorates the visit of Pope Pius VII in 1804 on Saint Dagobert's day, just prior to the pontiff's visit to the Razès.

Bérenger also spent time in the museum of the Louvre. After having informed himself concerning the painters of certain paintings, he purchased reproductions of three pictures, which on his return home he mounted on the walls of his humble lodgings. They were *The Arcadian Shepherds* by Poussin, the *Hermit Saint Anthony* by David Teniers, and a portrait of Pope Saint Celestine V from some unknown source. Truly these made a strange assortment.

While in Paris, Bérenger Saunière not only discovered painting but also music. Truly, Erato presented herself to him in some attractive guises. This era too, had its Callas. She bore the name of Emma Calvé. She was very beautiful and had made her debut nine years earlier at Brussels in Gounod's Faust. This twenty-four year old Marguerite created a sensation with her remarkable soprano voice and with her acting, which was filled with audacity. She had recently returned from London, hailed as the greatest living prima donna. The Queen, having heard her sing Carmen, had invited her to Windsor and had persuaded her to allow a bust to be carved.

At this time she was in Paris between two triumphant tours, and Massenet had composed Sappho especially for her. However since he had only just arrived in the capital, how the impoverished Curé of Rennes-le-Château was ever admitted to the presence of this diva we shall never know[1]. But the fact remains that the meeting took place, perhaps because the singer was so warm-hearted as to wish to prove to him that, except when on the stage, she had

---

1. Perhaps it was Hoffet who arranged the meeting between Emma Calvé and Saunière. Hoffet and the singer were in fact both intimate friends of the composer Claude Debussy, at whose house Emma and Bérenger might perhaps have met.

nothing in common with the poetess of Lesbos. Their relationship was seen and noted by everyone and was destined to last for several years.

However Bérenger did not forget the main object of his important journey. On the appointed day he returned to Abbé Bieil to learn what decision he had reached. It has not been possible to establish with certainty what was said and what passed between the two men. It certainly seems that Saunière was not handed back the manuscripts or else that he was only given some of them. Whatever may have happened, the matter later became somewhat clearer, since Mgr. Billard felt it advisable in March 1901 to make the journey to Saint-Sulpice in order to attempt to elucidate the problem. Had there been some transaction, resulting in the Curé parting with his precious documents in exchange for certain explanations not any less precious? If this was indeed the case, the course of events was to show that the price paid would later seem relatively trifling to our pilgrim.

ooOOoo

After three weeks stay so pleasantly occupied, Bérenger Saunière returned to his native district. At Carcassonne he made a more or less exact report to his bishop, who repaid him two thousand francs which was something more than was needed to reimburse the mayor, who was to be informed that the documents had been sold.

As soon as he had returned from his travels, the Curé recommenced his tasks. Aided by several young men, one of whom, Antoine Verdier is still alive, he first shifted the flagstone set at the foot of the high altar. It was then perceived that the newly exposed stone face was engraved. Known as "The Chevalier's Stone", this very ancient relic of Merovingian or Carolingian origin is now installed in the museum at Carcassonne. It comprises two panels, one of which is badly disfigured; but on the other can still be distinguished, either two knights astride the same horse or perhaps a knight at the gallop bearing in one hand a sceptre while the other supports a child upon the horse's neck.

In the space thus cleared, Saunière directed that a trench be dug to a depth of about a metre. But he then released his workmen, stating that the luncheon hour had arrived. He therefore remained alone within the church. However, the workmen had enough time to notice at the bottom of the trench two skeletons[1], and to catch sight of an earthenware jar filled with shining objects, which Saunière claimed were only medals and of no value.

From such scraps of evidence, it is apparent that at this time the Curé excavated at various locations in the church and there found several objects, the value of which should not, however, be over estimated. As was said

---

1. In the course of a new excavation carried out some years ago, the sepulchre has revealed a very singular skull that we shall discuss in more detail later.

by a learned man[1] who had studied the whole business,

"It was not the treasure but only a small hoard."

However, this was also the time when Abbé Saunière undertook, by himself, a most singular task and in a characteristic manner. Each day, accompanied by his faithful Marie, who was then irreverently known as his Madonna, he left the village carrying a basket upon his back. The couple wandered for a long time over the plateau, covering several kilometres each journey.

From a distance Bérenger could sometimes be perceived bending down, gathering up a stone, examining it and then either putting it into his basket or else flinging it away with disdain. In the evening he would return, bowed down under his load. Volunteering the information, he would explain to those intrigued by his strange actions:

"In order to decorate the little garden surrounding our cemetery I wish to construct a grotto of rocks, which will have a most pleasant appearance. For this purpose I must have a quantity of selected stones. Helped by Marie, I have to go quite a long way to find them. To this task I shall devote all the time that is needed."

Everybody was satisfied with this explanation, since Saunière did in fact build the grotto, stone by stone with his own hands. This baroque monument is still in existence, but is no longer as it used to be, since unknown folk have plundered much of it over the years, which comes as a great disappointment to the curious visitor.

---

1. René Descadeillas. *Notes on Rennes-le-Château and on Abbé Saunière.*

But what Bérenger found more difficult to explain was the reason why he spent his nights shut up in the cemetery.

There, close to the church, used to stand two tombstones, which marked the grave of Marie de Negri d'Ables, the wife of François d'Hautpoul, Marquis of Blanchefort and Seigneur of Rennes. This lady died shortly before the Revolution, and the Curé, Antoine Bigou, her chaplain and confessor has lovingly composed her epitaph.

Now if Bérenger Saunière loved stones to the extent of carrying them in full baskets on his back, it is hard to believe that these two stones, for some reason or other, were not suited to his purpose. For not only did he arrange to transport them from one end of the cemetery to the other, but with the aid of a quarry-man's tools, even patiently polished one stone until the inscriptions had been completely erased. Again, a little later, he caused the other stone to disappear.

This time however, his actions did cause some protest, since, even in the eyes of the most unbelieving, tombs are sacred. Besides, in the cemetery the Curé is not entirely in charge. In 1895 the municipality therefore informed Saunière that he was to leave the dead to sleep in peace.

Some while later the engineer Ernest Cros, a devotee of archaeology then stationed in the district, questioned Saunière on the matter.

"Why then, M. Curé, have you displaced this tomb?"

"You see, several parishioners die every year, and the cemetery has become too small for them to have proper burials. I have therefore provided the ossuary that you see here, for the more ancient remains. I must ensure that it is well covered over. That is what I intend to use this tombstone for."

"But how can it be that a man such as you, being so cultivated, so knowledgeable of the past, should have obliterated this antique inscription?"

"On an ossuary, it would have had no significance," was Bérenger's evasive reply, whereupon he quickly changed the subject.

But what Saunière did not know, is that he had undertaken a task or taken a precaution, which was completely futile. In fact, before he had effected their disappearance, the inscriptions so tritely carved on the tomb of the Marchioness de Blanchefort had been noted in the course of excursions made by local archaeologists. One has accordingly been reproduced in the *Bulletin de la Société des Études Scientifiques de l'Aude* while the other features in the now very rare work of Eugène Stublein, *Engraved stones of Languedoc.*

The first, on a slab set vertically, appeared as shown overleaf in Fig.1. The other slab was rectangular and was laid at the foot of the first. Remnants of this second slab are still to be found in the cemetery at Rennes-le-Château. It once bore the inscription shown in Fig.2.

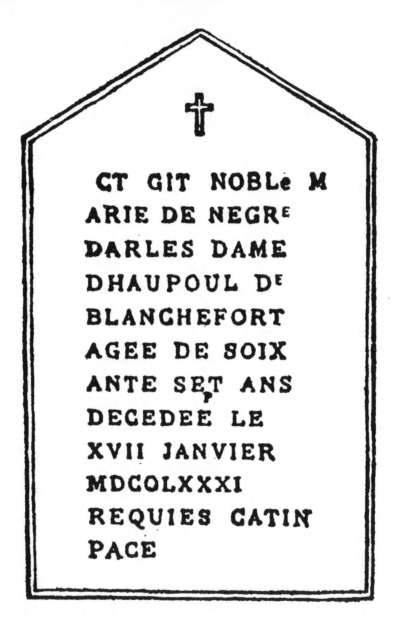

Fig. 1. Headstone.

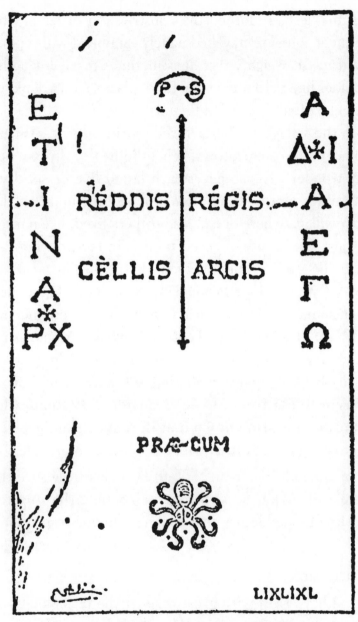

Fig. 2. Gravestone copied by Eugène Stublein.
Supplied by M.R. Chésa.

After he had finished the construction of his grotto, Bérenger Saunière travelled widely. Supplied with a port-manteau (so weighty that he sometimes carried it on his shoulder like a cross and sometimes placed it on a donkey's neck) he often descended the tortuous pathway that leads from the village to the civilised world outside. Where did he go? No one knows. What did he do? In vain one may wonder. His absences each lasted five or six days, sometimes more. If he often stopped at Montazels, his native village where one of his brothers lived, like himself a Priest, he hardly lingered there. In fact, during this period he sent to various persons, letters that he posted in the outlying towns, Perpignan, Nice, Lons-le-Saunier, Valenciennes... Also there is available his correspondence with a Paris banking house, Petitjean Bank, Rue Montmartre, wherein various transactions are mentioned in guarded words by both parties. This bank even sent one of its representatives, M. de Beauvière, to Rennes-le-Château. It is also known that Bérenger Saunière was in close communication with a jeweller of Mazamet.

In any case our man took great pains to ensure the secrecy of his journeys. Before each of them, he prepared a series of typed letters in which his humour is apparent:

Rennes-le-Château.

Dear Sir,

I have read with great respect the letter that you have kindly sent me and to which I am giving much attention. Believe me, the question that you have presented to me does not completely escape me but does deserve my further consideration. Thus I trust that you will allow me to deal with my urgent business and I shall be able to answer you in a few days time.

Yours,

B. Saunière, Priest.

These letters were usually addressed to the Bishop, to his chancellor or else to the Vicar-General, also to neighbouring clergy. Only one of the pair was obliged to put in an appearance. The faithful Marie Denarnaud had only the date to add, since the postmark would be sufficient guarantee that our Curé (gone one knows not where) had not left the region; the ploy had succeeded!

At the same time the orders poured in upon Marie. They were sent from Germany, Spain, Switzerland and Italy, sometimes by religious communities and amounting to an hundred or one hundred and fifty francs each day. And at this point, Bérenger Saunière, who such a short time before had been reduced to his last centime, rushed into expenditure, follies and extravagances. First of all, in 1896 he undertook to repair the church out of his own pocket. This time it was no longer a matter of minor works. He would rebuild the edifice from top to bottom. Under his direct supervision, a gang of workmen shifted or raised some of the windows and added to the sacristy a small back room accessed through a secret door concealed by a panel. He also cut through a wall so as to install a staircase leading up to the pulpit. Sometimes the design of the builder was not apparent to those who had to carry out the work.

Why for example was it necessary to install at the head of the nave and near the entrance, sixty-four square tiles, alternately black and white? But Saunière was the authority and personally supervised everything down to the finest detail. There was no question of discussing the plans. Besides, what was the point, since he was paying on the nail for everything?

The Curé then engaged, fed and lodged, again all at his expense, a team of sculptors and painters, though we know not from where, and set them to work on the interior and exterior decoration of the church. The artists stayed on for several months and carried out work on the tympanum over the doorway, statues, pictures, stained glass windows, the Stations of the Cross and the pulpit.

Once again Saunière, that patron of barbaric but fastidious taste, was the inspiration and master workman. He composed all the inscriptions himself and caused the Calvary to be rebuilt three times as he was not satisfied with the angle of the head of Christ. This Calvary alone cost eleven thousand francs. On some occasions Bérenger himself took up the palette and paintbrush. The Madeleine painted under the altar is entirely his work.

The entire work was finished in 1897. Bérenger soon invited his Bishop to witness its inauguration. Mgr. Billard should logically have rejoiced unreservedly at the work of his subordinate, who, without asking a penny from his superiors, had in so short a time restored the ruins of the buildings belonging to the church. However, as soon as he arrived, the prelate was overcome by an indefinable uneasiness, the same that all will experience who enter this strange sanctuary. Even though he was accustomed to the hideous imagery of the period, could he have considered, like Léon Bloy, that ugliness is in itself blasphemous? Or perhaps he felt trapped by the spell of the bizarre world conjured up by Bérenger?

It would seem here that Saunière had indulged in a malicious play upon words in carving on the tympanum arch the fearful cry of Jacob at Bethel, "Terribilis est locus iste". Yes, this place is truly terrible.

Perhaps again when reading another inscription,

"Mea domus orationis vocabitur." (My house is called a house of prayer) did the prelate recall what followed this evangelical quotation,

"Now you have made of it a den of thieves," and just about grasped the allusion. In any case, he could not stomach what he saw. He hastened to leave the church, quickly blessing the Calvary; he murmured a few polite words and departed. In future Rennes-le-Château was to be excluded from his pastoral visits.

But for Saunière the craving for further building was far from being satisfied. In 1900 he bought up a wide tract of land extending up to the edge of the peak of red and white rock upon which stands the village. The site is superb, commanding a view as far as the eye can see. There above the abyss he caused to be erected the crenellated tower in two stories, which he called the Tour Magdala or Magdala tower; the lower hall was his private room wherein only those invited might enter, while in the upper portion his library was installed.

As always, the builders served only as the docile craftsmen, since Saunière himself was the real architect. Thus, although stones were not lacking roundabout, yet it was necessary to bring those suitable for his purpose from a great distance on mule-back, without worrying about the cost of transport or the difficulties. With a mathematician's precision he personally supervised the aspect of the tower. He traced out the fortified walkway, in the form of the arc of a circle, from which the countryside in all its aspects can be admired as one walks. At the other end of his domain he had built the spacious villa, which he called Bethania. Then he constructed the orangery and designed the park with its paths and the formal ponds, which were fed from three immense cisterns.

Archaeologists who visited the site sung high praises:

We were welcomed by M. l'Abbé Saunière. He took pleasure in letting us visit his fine estate, which without fear of contradiction, seems like a lost oasis in the midst of a desert. There is a level area occupied by a kitchen garden wherein are grown vegetables that would make any market gardener jealous. Then there is an orchard and a fine pleasure garden sheltered by a terrace from which a marvellous view may be enjoyed.

To the south there is a tower, which seems to stand guardian over this charming corner: it was in these restful surroundings that we lingered, savouring a few minutes relaxation while admiring the rich library that had been installed therein[1].

---

1. A.Fages, *Bulletin de la Société des Études Scientifiques de l'Aude*. Volume XX, 1909.

This estate might well be the cause for some pride. It had cost about a million francs.

More surprising still was the life-style, which henceforth was enjoyed by Bérenger. To him, Magdala was doubly his ivory tower. There, far from the vain disturbances of the world, he would no doubt contemplate thus:

"Let the ignorant man return to his learning, and the fisherman to his net." Bethany on the other hand was to be his regal court, the Lord's house, open to all, where visitors would find clean beds and a well-furnished table. A hospitable house, which soon became the target of the scandalmongers.

In fact it appeared as if Bérenger Saunière had at his disposal inexhaustible resources as he gave free rein to all the caprices of his fantastic imagination. Not content with being provided with the library that he had so long dreamed of, he engaged a bookbinder from Toulouse to work for him over many months. He also installed in this building on a permanent basis, a photographer to take pictures of all the noteworthy places in the neighbourhood. He made one collection of ten thousand postcards and another of one hundred thousand stamps. He also collected ancient pieces of furniture, fabrics and pottery. The company of his two dogs, Faust and Pomponnet, was not enough for him. So he built a zoological garden and populated it with fish, peacocks, monkeys and parrots. The ducks in his poultry yard were even spoon-fed on biscuits.

"He who lives in the land of the cassoulet (Languedoc) must order his beans from Lille."

These fantasies, just as childish as they were costly, still amaze those who knew him in those days of ostentation.

The villa Bethania was never empty. One could see there in close company, preachers like the Priest Ferrafiat; regional notables; people invited from Paris such as the Secretary of State for Fine Arts; Dujardin-Baumetz; beautiful ladies and grande dames: Emma Calvé certainly, but also that lady of letters, Andrée Bruguière who did not hesitate to have herself addressed as Viscountess of Artois, and the quite authentic Marchioness of Bozas. The most mysterious guest was he whom the villagers were reduced to calling "The Foreigner", though behind this incognito was concealed the Archduke John of Hapsburg, cousin to the Emperor of Austro-Hungaria.

All was provided to ensure for this motley company an enchanting stay: a servant in white apron and laundered head-dress would serve Marsala, Malvoisie and Tokay. The drinks flowed freely, as Saunière's accounts bore witness:

1st November 1900.

1 barrel of Martinique Rum in case ABC No. 1031.
   45 litres @ 2 francs = 90 francs.

50 litres of rum @ 2.35 francs = 117.50 francs,
   (Rum perfect, almost historic).

33 litres of white wine Haut Barsac.

35 litres of Malvoisie.

17 litres of Golden Cinchona.

53 litres of Banyuls.

12 litres of Muscatel.

Had Marie then ceased being jealous? She certainly seems to have resigned herself without overmuch trouble to seeing, by this sudden change of fortune, so many petticoats around Bérenger. Perhaps it was her peasant philosophy; perhaps she was flattered by the rapid ascent of the man with whom she had shared so much hardship. High Society might well judge her as being somewhat simple minded, but she knew herself to be irreplaceable. Nobody knew Saunière as she knew him. No one else had travelled, or ever would travel along that fantastic road at his side.

To be just, one must admit that the voluptuous Curé did much good to those around him, even if he remains bizarre in the various diversions that he offered to his parishioners. The famous Visigothic pillar of the high altar he had transported to the church square, not without first having a portion polished smooth and engraved with the inscription, MISSION 1891. Upon this he had mounted the semblance of an ugly cake decoration, the Virgin of Lourdes, who, while offering advice to her devotees, only too clearly demonstrated Bérenger's sense of humour; PÉNITENCE! PÉNITENCE! The villagers would have found his taste all the more ambiguous, since in the Aude people were living very frugally at that time.

It did not matter so much, however, since the Curé had granted an annual rent of five thousand francs to the municipality and had given to the poorest families sums of ten to fifteen thousand francs, which at that time amounted to small fortunes.

And again, the inauguration of the monument was a memorable occasion. At the time of unveiling the pillar, there gushed forth an impressive display of fireworks. Also Saunière had placed innumerable firecrackers, linked by a fuse, all around the courtyard. Their salvos re-echoed for several leagues roundabout.

So things continued to go well with the Curé. Besides, though a Priest might be harshly judged in the country where he is still remembered as a "Holy Terror", the people of the anti-clerical Midi are indulgent towards the weaknesses of mankind. So at Rennes-le-Château this is not so paradoxical as it might appear. Abbé Saunière has above all left behind the memory of scarcely an ordinary fellow, but one who had a notoriously devil-may-care personality. Certainly he has loosened many tongues and has set imaginations working; but in this wilderness, where distractions are rare, his life, his caprices, follies and baroque ideas showed more than a grain of the unexpected.

Every day there was a spectacle for which he had created the scenery and for which he was at the same time producer, director and principal star. Above all, he was loved because he was typical of the Languedoc where no virtues are held in more esteem than disinterested cordiality and generous elegance even though they may be tinged with ostentation.

What is more surprising, is that the ecclesiastical authorities in no way hastened to interfere with the strange doings of the Abbé Saunière. Just as they had shut their eyes to his liaison with a servant only eighteen years old, they would wish to ignore the follies at the villa Bethania. They did not even enquire into the origin of the resources that made it possible for the Curé to follow so sumptuous a lifestyle. In those days it is true, Bishops had many other cares. The law concerning congregations had just been passed, and disestablishment was imminent, relations with the State being stretched to the extreme. Perhaps Mgr. Billard also had good reasons to be circumspect with his problem child.

But in 1902, Mgr. de Beauséjour succeeded Mgr. Billard in the Episcopal office at Carcassonne and the following year Pius X succeeded Leo XIII on the pontifical throne. For Bérenger Saunière everything was changed at a stroke.

The new Bishop wisely proceeded by stages. He first directed Bérenger to go for a few weeks into retreat at a convent, but it was soon necessary to adopt other measures to curb a nature cast in such a mould. In January 1908 he offered him the parish of Coustauge; the Charterhouse of Durban was near at hand and one would imagine this environment would suffice to disturb our Priest. Saunière therefore took up his finest pen and replied insolently to his Bishop,

"I cannot leave a parish where my interests keep me."

In fact, to which interests did he refer? Mgr. de Beauséjour decided it would be better to summon the Curé to Carcassonne, but alas Bérenger was indisposed.

Yet the number of illnesses matched the number of proposed meetings. Each time, fortunately, a medical certificate accompanied the letter of excuses. These certificates were mere sops, sent by Dr. Rocher of Couiza who wrote thus to Saunière:

"Dear friend, I enclose the certificate you requested. If it is not adequate, let me know what you need and I shall be pleased to give you satisfaction."

If his diplomatic illnesses prevented Bérenger from presenting himself at Carcassonne, they certainly made it possible for him to pursue his escapades abroad under the cover of the ingenious postal system operated with the complicity of Marie.

But after a year of this little game, Saunière was no longer able to avoid making a visit to the episcopal palace.

"You seem to require a much grander style than I," said Mgr. de Beauséjour, "and I wish to have a statement of the origin of your resources which seem so sudden and important."

"Alas Monseigneur you ask of me the only thing that I am not able to reveal. Deep sinners to whom, with the aid of God, I have shown the way of penitence have given these considerable amounts to me. You will yourself understand that I would not wish to betray the secrets of the confessional by giving you their names."

The bishop could have retorted that, while exhorting other folk to penitence, his visitor certainly did not lack self-possession himself. But the argument behind the cunning Curé's thrust went without riposte. In fact, each of the participants did well and won the respect of his adversary.

"So be it, I shall respect your scruples. But if you are not able to tell me anything as to the source of your finances, enlighten me at least as to their employment."

"I could not let you see the accounts, Monseigneur since the donors have made me the sole judge as to the best use of their money for they have given it to me personally and not to the church. If they continue to show themselves to be so generous, is that not proof enough that I have not abused their confidence? Why then do you reproach me? My parish, when I first arrived was in a lamentable state. I have rebuilt and beautified the church without asking a centime from the diocese. I deserve your congratulations rather than your suspicions."

"After all," insolently declared Saunière, "it is to my superiors upon whom the duty should rightly fall to ensure for Rennes-le-Château a church that is worthy of the faithful and a decent dwelling for the pastor."

"It must only be a hindrance that the luxury of your establishment has become the object of scandal."

"If nothing has seemed too good for me, Monseigneur," replied the Curé with pride, "it is because these buildings will become a home of retreat for elderly Priests after my death."

The Bishop did not persist in the wrangle. But some time later he ordered Saunière to submit, in writing, an exact statement of his expenditure. We have held in our own hands the laboured rough copy of the memoir, which the Curé submitted. With the aid of much cheating he succeeded in bringing the cost of his construction work down to one hundred and ninety-three thousand francs. This sum was by no means modest (bearing in mind for comparison that the yearly salary of an ambassador was at that time some forty thousand francs) but this did not in fact represent one fifth of Bérenger Saunière's actual expenditure. Thus, the whole of the furniture was put at a figure of ten thousand francs, though his bookcases in solid oak would alone have reached that figure. It is believed that no presentable receipts were attached to the memorandum. The Curé, who for his own petty expenses put down everything to the nearest centime, pretended that he was not familiar with accounting.

Tired of being flouted, Mgr. de Beauséjour then changed his tactics.

"These resources, for which you cannot declare the source," said he to Saunière, "have been drawn by you, from a traffic in Masses."

Our hero then took a certain pleasure in justifying himself. At that time a Mass would have cost about fifty centimes. Without dispensation a Priest had not the right to celebrate more than three Masses in a single day. One hundred and ninety three thousand francs would mean three hundred and eighty six thousand Masses. To pronounce them, Saunière would need to have lived some three hundred and fifty years. And furthermore it would have been necessary for each one of his parishioners to have obtained from him more than three thousand Masses.

What then to do next? The Bishop decided that he must break the indomitable Curé. Persisting in his accusation of simony, he brought the case before his superiors of the Ecclesiastical Court. Through his failure to attend, Saunière caused the proceedings to hang out for six months. On the 5th December 1910, the ecclesiastical judges declared him to be "Suspens a divinis". In plain terms this meant that he no longer had the right to perform Mass or to administer the sacraments.

But far from bending, the Curé of Rennes-le-Château in 1911 threw in an appeal to Rome. His advocate, Canon Huguet of the diocese of Agen spent two years at the Vatican at Saunière's expense, showing the fallacious and improbable nature of the accusation of the traffic in Masses. In 1913, Mgr. Beauséjour's claim was dismissed[1]. Bérenger had won his case.

This success was however short lived. Through some unknown channel, an important Vatican personality

---

1. At the bishopric of Carcassonne, there are those who deny that the Saunière case was ever sent to Rome. Nevertheless certain documents of Roman law are to be found in the private archives of a collector, M. Noël Corbu.

was informed that behind this local chicanery the stable concealed a much larger horse of an entirely different colour. Rome encouraged the Bishop of Carcassonne to put forward a counter-appeal. On the 11th April 1915, without any new charge being invoked against him the Curé of Rennes-le-Château was definitely suspended. He was accordingly summoned to give up the presbytery and church to his successor Abbé Henri Marty.

This was bad news for Saunière. In 1905 the law of disestablishment had been passed, so that churches and presbyteries had become communal amenities. A little while afterwards Bérenger (a one-time reactionary who was by then mixing frequently with prominent radicals) hired out to the municipality the presbytery, this being under the name of Marie. The new Curé was therefore forced to dwell down in the plain some kilometres distant. Hence on Sundays after he had clambered up to the village, all sweating and puffing, he found himself preaching to empty pews. The real Mass, that which everyone attended, was the one that Saunière, since there was no other suitable building close by, conducted in the chapel that he set up right next to his villa.

His quarrels with the hierarchy had deprived him of a favourable obscurity and then the war, which caused the frontiers to be closed, interfered with Bérenger's activities, which by that time needed more journeys and more money. In 1911, he sought a loan from the Credit

Foncier and toyed with selling part of his assets. In 1915 the cabinetmaker, who had built all his furniture to order, laid claim to a heavy bill of sale yet unpaid.

Then came the blow of his severance from the church, and the virtuous ones, as so often happens in such circumstances, sought to administer the final blow. This was at a time when counter-espionage flourished.

"Keep silent, beware, enemy ears are listening." Due to his strange life style Saunière was naturally the target of suspicion. Some whispered that he was a German agent and that his villa served as a relay station for the secret service of the Kaiser. Folk even went so far as to suggest that within his tower was concealed a cannon.

But one must believe that this clever devil would quickly find a remedy for his money troubles. In fact he soon planned new projects, more romantic, more enormous than ever. Since he desired to possess a motorcar but at that time no road existed that was passable for vehicles, he arranged for the construction of a roadway four kilometres in length to connect Rennes-le-Château to Couiza. He also decided to install running water for all the inhabitants of the village, which he intended to encircle with ramparts as in the past.

He planned the construction of a new chapel, placed at the centre of the cemetery and provided with a baptismal font as was customary with the early Christians. But he had even more ambitious ideas. He ordered the construction

of a tower seventy metres in height, the interior walls of
which were to be lined with books from floor to ceiling.
This library of Babel, worthy of the imagination of
the Borgias, was approached by a spiral staircase. At the
summit the Abbé, like a muezzin, would proclaim to
the faithful the new religious ideas that were beginning to
germinate within his brain.

Were these just the dreams of megalomania? Not at all.
He first had the architect Caminade draw up plans for these
wonderful constructions. (Stolen by someone unknown,
these plans vanished in 1930). Then on the 15th January
l917 he signed the estimate for the work to be carried out
by the contractor Elie Bot, which work would cost eight
million Napoleons, or eighteen million new francs.

But Bérenger Saunière had not the time to realise these
grandiose projects. Two days later on the 17th January he
was struck by an apoplectic fit at the doorway of the
Magdala tower. A surgeon from Carcassonne, Doctor
Courrent, who was also an archaeologist, came to his
bedside. The patient was vigorous, but he had burned the
candle at both ends. Perhaps he could not be cured.

Bérenger Saunière finally yielded up his spirit on 22nd
January 1917 at the age of sixty-five. His body tarried as a
silent sentinel on the ramparts of his walkway, where his
earthly remains were set up in state, draped in a covering
adorned with red tassels. All the villagers filed past to
render him their final homage. In remembrance each
one plucked a tassel as a keep-sake to take away. He was
interred in the cemetery where he had spent so many nights

in order to obliterating an epitaph. No-one came to lay flowers on his tomb, which soon became jealously guarded by the brambles.

When he felt that his end was nigh, Bérenger had sent for Abbé Rivière, the Curé of the neighbouring village Esperaza. This man, a lover of high living, was his long-time friend and had not broken with him when he was placed under an interdiction. Having a broad outlook he knew the weakness of the flesh and believed in God's indulgence towards prodigal sons. What passed between the two Priests? We shall never know. But when Rivière left his dying friend he was deathly pale and thrown into confusion.

His emotion was not transitory. He became withdrawn, taciturn and silent. Up to his death, he was not seen to laugh. What terrible secrets had been imparted to him in confidence? What spiritual abyss had he seen gaping before him? Did Bérenger's soul seem to have already changed into one of those stones on which even divine mercy had broken its wings? Did he think that he had abandoned his friend on the very threshold of hell?

Anyway, something happened that had never been seen before: it was not until two days after he died, that the Curé of Rennes-le-Château received the last sacraments from the hands of Abbé Rivière. Right up to the end and even after, Bérenger Saunière was thus able to maintain his aura of mystery.

However, he does not seem to have the makings of one of the great damned souls. Under the Second Empire what could better benefit a poor family of four children than a little boy of intelligence who might well become an ecclesiastic? It was unfortunate that Bérenger was born to be an adventurer, explorer, man of affairs, pirate, or soldier, anything but a Priest. When his superiors became aware of this, did they think to change him by exiling him upon a forgotten rock? Did these men, who by their profession appeared so very prudent, really examine him closely enough? Could none of them see the energy and boundless acquisitiveness expressed in his countenance? Did they not detect in him something of the soldier of fortune, the blood of the terrible mercenaries of ancient Aragon? He brought to Rennes-le-Château all the accumulated desires of a poor child, from the toys he had vainly coveted to the riches far out of his reach. All the amusements of the village had passed him by as his seminarist's robe had prevented him from competing with other boys at shooting, drinking or mixing with the girls.

As he advanced in age and in learning, his desires only multiplied and became more complex. So who would have directed, to the damnation of Bérenger Saunière, those disorganised appetites which were seething with vitality? What Mephistopheles, disguised perhaps as one of his dogs Faust or Pomponnet, would have revealed to him the realisation of his youthful dreams?

The close of the nineteenth century seems to us so uninteresting that we sometimes forget the extent to which it was haunted by the devil. Bloy and Huysmans bear witness to this obsession. And even Barrès felt his influence. By the way, have you read *La Colline Inspirée?*

At the death of Bérenger Saunière, his books, pictures, a large portion of his papers and even certain of the stones with which he had populated his domain disappeared[1] as if by magic. When they came to examine, with an impatience that can be well imagined, the will of this man who had thrown millions of gold pieces out of the window, his heirs and the bishopric were dumbfounded. The Curé possessed nothing, and had never possessed anything; all his effects both movable and fixed, belonged to Marie Denarnaud, his servant.

Bethany was closed. Those who had once been received there, hastened to erase every trace of this from their memory. Did not the Christ of The Sacré-Coeur, which dominates the pediment, open his arms as widely to bid farewell to those who were leaving, as to welcome those who would enter? The iron gate of the portal opened as easily in one direction as in the other.

ooOOoo

---

1. One portion of his library appears to have been broken up by the Gacon Library at Lyon; as regards the second Visigothic pillar of the altar, this would seem to have been placed near Millau by Emma Calvé.

PART TWO

THE GOLD OF RENNES

While following with us Bérenger Saunière's foolish extravagances, the reader must surely have considered whether he should evaluate the cost in gold francs, since the gold franc (or Napoleon) is equivalent to 2.20 of our new francs.

Thus, when considering the false account that he presented to his Bishop, Bérenger, on his own admission, would have spent for the civil works and the initial repairs carried out in the church alone some four hundred and twenty five thousand of our francs. As one commentator emphasised,

"It is a question of a considerable sum for those days."[1] But we know from the invoices that this work in reality cost one million and thirty thousand new francs.

---

1. René Descadeillas. *Note on Rennes-le-Château and on Abbé Saunière.*

To that must be added the cost for the entire decoration of the church. Here the bulk of the accountable receipts are not available. But since the Calvary alone cost eleven thousand gold francs (say, twenty four thousand, two hundred new francs) one can estimate without any great error that the entire decoration, being as we have seen, terribly expensive, would have cost about five hundred thousand francs.

It is also necessary to take into account the ostentatious style of living of the Curé who kept open house for more than ten years from the time of his discovery until he wearied of wealth. In order to achieve this, three thousand francs per month would seem a reasonable estimate, making a total over ten years of three hundred and sixty thousand francs.

But there are also excellent reasons for believing that the Curé of Rennes-le-Château sent to Mgr. Billard a sum of one million gold francs with which the Bishop undertook to restore the Dominican monastery of Prouilles. Finally, one can hardly imagine that Bérenger would have signed, shortly prior to his sudden death, a contract for eight million gold francs if he did not have access to adequate funds to cover that amount.

So, between 1891 and 1917, our hero would have disposed of an amount, in total, of between a minimum of fifteen million and a maximum of twenty-four million gold francs. Expressed in old francs this sum would fall between one and a half milliards and two milliards four hundred millions of old francs!

However, no matter whether it was one and a half milliard or two milliards[1] four hundred millions, sums of this magnitude must inevitably lead one to ask from whence came the sudden enrichment of the poverty-stricken Abbé Saunière.

These figures must first of all completely rule out the accusation as to traffic in Masses advanced by Mgr. de Beauséjour, since this would have implied that Saunière had recruited his clients from the whole of France by widespread advertisements. To support such an allegation, not a scrap of evidence existed. Furthermore, the Bishop later confided to one of his friends, Mgr. de Cabrières,

"It served my purpose, but I never believed it." The accusation was so feeble that when it was submitted to Rome it was not given serious consideration, as we have seen: we need not discuss it any further.

It was also suggested that the Curé's riches were derived from the generosity of Emma Calvé. This explanation is no more credible than the previous theory.

In fact, although it was common knowledge, the liaison between Bérenger and the singer was only intermittent. A meeting in Paris, a few visits by Emma to Rennes-le-Château, and that is all. During the period when Saunière lived on the grand scale, Emma Calvé was for four years absent in the United States; while in 1914 she put an end to the liaison by marrying the tenor Gasbarri. One can

---

1. Translation note: One milliard is equal to one thousand million. 15,000,000 gold francs = 1,500,000,000 old francs = 33,000,000 new (or heavy) francs.

hardly imagine that, three years later, she would promise to finance any of the works that the Curé planned to undertake. After all it is quite unjustified to attribute to the singer such unbounded resources and prodigality and to our hero such an objectionable character.

There only remains the common folk's explanation, that which you will hear in the neighbourhood, and the one that the reader has already divined. Bérenger Saunière had discovered a treasure, one so fabulous that it was far from having been exhausted when he was overtaken by his death. The most singular aspect of the affair under consideration is that when the subject is closely scrutinised, this explanation is the only one that is in accordance with certain facts.

Shortly before the Saunière era, the tableland of Rennes became the theatre for extraordinary discoveries. First there was the discovery of a mixture of Arab gold coins weighing nearly twenty kilograms in all. Then in 1860 a farmer named Rougé found a fifty kilogram gold ingot covered in bituminous material, made at a place called "Charbonnières", situated near Bézu.

As to Saunière, on one occasion he presented a chalice, which was extremely fine and very ancient, to his friend Abbé Grassaud, Curé of Saint-Paul-de-Fenouillet (Pyrénées-Orientales). The family of the recipient still retains this example of the goldsmith's skill.

He also gave coins and ancient jewels to several families in the neighbourhood and these have been preserved. One of his protégés, the schoolmaster Jammes, was so richly endowed that he was able to purchase an estate.

In 1928, after Saunière's death, there was discovered in a ruined hut by the side of the Couleurs stream near Rennes-le-Château, a massive gold statuette that had been partly melted, though the feet could still be distinguished. This find occurred close to where was discovered a crucible, still bearing traces of molten gold, at Saunière's birthplace in Montazels.

All these facts throw some light on his strange roaming over the mountain under the pretext of gathering stones, his frequent journeys to distant parts, his relations with a bank and with a jeweller, together with his obstinate evasions when he was challenged to explain the source of his sudden fortune

However, on one occasion Bérenger broke this silence through a remark that he made in semi-confidence. When his friend, Antoine Beaux, Curé of Campagne-sur-Aude, said to him, half-jokingly,

"My dear fellow, seeing you living in such magnificent style leads one to think that you have unearthed a treasure." He looked him straight in the eyes, and in the langue d'oc he replied as follows, enunciating every word,

"*Me l'han donat, l'hay panat, l'hay parat e bé le téni.*"

"It was shown to me, I put my hand upon it, I have worked it all out and I am holding it firmly."

He did not say any more, and never returned to the subject, at least not openly. But one can assume that he did allude to it, though in a veiled symbolic manner, in his intimate memorandum. We have held this faded exercise book in our hands and it begins in a very strange manner.

The flyleaf is covered with two pictures cut out from the journal, *La Croix*. The first represents three angels with a child in a shroud and is accompanied by this legend:

"The year 1891 passed into eternity with the fruits to be spoken of below." Under this there has been pasted a picture showing the adoration of the magi bearing the words: "Receive O King, gold, the symbol of royalty." These collages are all the stranger because the journal proper, which is set out with a precise and diligent pen, does not commence until May 1901. And except for detailed information as to building work, presents hardly anything of interest. But the year 1891, which bore gold as its fruit, is exactly the time when Bérenger found the documents that turned him into a rich man.

Among Bérenger Saunière's personal papers we have also found this strange cryptogram:

```
YE NS Z N U M G L N Y Y R F V H E N M Z F
P ● S O T +  P E C H E U R + A + L ' E M B Z
V O U C H U R E + D U + R H O N E , S O N Z
U P O I S S O N + S U R + L E + G R I L + F
L D E U X +  F O I S + R E T O U R N A. U D
R N + M A L I N + S U R V I N T + E T + X H
R X V + F O I S + L E + G O U T A + . C U Z
T I T ., I L + N E + L U I + R E S T A + Q V
K U E + L ' A R E T E . + U N + A N G E + T
N V E I L L A I T + E T + E N + F I T + U Q
Y N P E I G N E + D ' O R . B . S . C U R H
O V T S V K Y R M S T I J P Z C K P F X K A
```

Fig. 3. Abbé Bérenger Saunière's cryptogram.

If the Curé of Rennes-le-Château had in truth discovered a treasure, what could have been its origin and nature?

"Mystery" and "secret" are the words that most frequently recur from the pens of the few learned scholars who have been drawn towards the Razès and in particular towards Rennes.

When studying the origin of the most ancient inhabitants of the district, the historian R. Lizop states,

"Light has not yet been cast upon the problem posed by the mysterious old city of Reddae." Another historian Louis Fédié goes further;

"The founding of Rennes-le-Château is so mysterious that it seems to have discouraged the chroniclers and the archaeologists."

Finally as Abbé Mazières has stated,

"It is a land famous for its legends, its traditions, its secrets, its enigmas and for a whole series of discoveries, some of which are sensational."

To attempt to throw some light upon this remote patch of country where Bérenger Saunière lived out his extraordinary adventure, we must dig into its legends and also its history. These two studies, far from being mutually exclusive, are in fact complementary.

We need not reject legends out-of-hand, just because their appeal seems superficial. They do not contradict matters of historical fact, but rather signal their presence. Like conventional road signs, it would seem that they could indicate symbolically the right route to those who have learned to read them, even over an unknown territory.

Not only are legends often based on historical facts whose traces they help to uncover, but also we know from Marx and Freud, that the products of the human imagination, even the most fantastic, derive their forms and sense from the history of societies and individuals. Faced with these imaginary creations, the progress of the historian can and should run parallel with that of the psychoanalyst. By attacking folklore in the same way as the psychoanalyst attacks dreams, the historian must ascend like him, from his physical nature to his latent occult nature and raise the veil of symbols in order to extract their secrets.

For the legend resorts to the same obscuring processes as those employed by the dream. Such are the rebus, the play on words or pseudo-etymology, deliberate errors of detail, expression of apparent irrelevancies, inversions, etc.

This approach leads to certain conclusions. We know that the analysis of dreams can reveal events that have become repressed into the sub-conscious minds of those who once intentionally rejected them. In the same way, the analysis of legends can sometimes bring to light facts that have been lost from the conscious folk-memory and sometimes disclose facts that have been deliberately concealed. These two aspects of legend analysis often become entangled and we have to unravel the sections of pure folklore from those of a more knowing authorship. One can then see that the medium of fantasy always leads, cryptically but sometimes rapidly, from relevant traditions to factual outcomes. The rich legendry of the Razès will be found to shed the flickering light of a flaming torch upon a story richer still.

Its quite remarkable mineralogical and hydrographical characteristics have ensured that the Rennes-les-Bains/ Rennes-le-Château region was inhabited from a very early date. There one may find an abundance of rocks, metals and minerals upon which our ancestors wrought their skill — amber, jet, copper, lead, pyrites, galena, nickel, sulphur, saltpetre, silver and gold. The seams are often polar; that is to say, they are oriented with respect to the magnetic meridian. Also Rennes-les-Bains is situated on the principal meridian of Paris, which fact has not failed to give rise to supernatural speculations.

Rennes-le-Château possesses, under its ramparts, a spring that never runs dry. As to the springs at Rennes-les-Bains, of which mention has already been made, an old memoir informs us that,

> From time to time, out of the waters there emerges mercury. Also from these waters there has been extracted sodium carbonate, the true nitre[1] of the alchemists. The water additionally contains a small amount of bitumen.

---

1. Translation note: The reference to "the true nitre of the alchemists" seems to refer to the fact that the Greek for nitre (saltpetre, or potassium nitrate) is the same as that for sodium carbonate (natron or washing soda). The Greek word comes from the Arabic for sodium carbonate (natrûn). It was natron that was used by the ancient Egyptians for embalming.

It is a curious thing that the name of Rennes, which is common to the two localities of interest, has been derived from two different place-names. The name of Rennes-le-Château was formerly Aereda, later Reddae or Rhedae. The name from which comes Razès (Rhedesium) is, according to some, derived from Aer Red (the serpent runner, the Celtic or pre-Celtic god of lightning) while others quote the Visigothic word Rheda, meaning a chariot[1].

In contrast Rennes-les-Bains, first called Bains de Regnes whose springs have existed since antiquity, did not become an important town until much later. The name is derived from the Latin Regnum and the barbarian word Es or Is designating either water or else stone. Rennes therefore can mean either Royal Water or Royal Stone.

The region became populated at a very early date, as is evidenced by the statue of Isis and the votive inscriptions to the mother of the gods that were found at Rennes-les-Bains, and by the Neolithic ossuary discovered at Rennes-le-Château. Since that era the region has never ceased to be inhabited. After the Iberian settlement, at the end of the fourth century B.C. the mysterious tribe of the Rêdu (in Latin, Redones) dwelt there and has left its name in various places such as Camp Redon.

According to several historians this tribe belonged to the people of the Belgae, whose name signifies Bergers

---

1. According to the works of Louis Fédié and Abbé Lasserre, an altar to Aer Red has also been discovered in this region — Du Mège-*Pyrenean Archaeology* Vol. II. p.142. The association of serpent and chariot in the name of Rennes-le-Château has not failed to give rise to astronomical interpretations.

(Shepherds). Having been driven from the shores of the North Sea, this tribe became split into two groups, one of which settled in Brittany, the other in the Razès.

"It is strange," remarks one of the editors of the *General History of Languedoc*, "to see at the two ends of France the ethnic names Redensis and Redones, evidently borrowed from the same root, and leading in both cases to the modern name of Rennes." The theory that there were two settlements founded by the Rêdu has the merit of satisfactorily explaining this peculiarity.

Later, as has been pointed out by an ancient author,

"The Romans established themselves in this region, not because of its beauty, for nature has not endowed it with much charm, but by reason of the various minerals that occur there in quantity." The roman road to Spain passed through Rennes-le-Château and later became known as the Way of St Jacques. At Rennes-les-Bains the colonists built extremely luxurious thermal baths encrusted with gold and precious stones. The ruins of these baths may yet be seen.

This double purpose, mining and thermal springs, was all reflected, like the antiquity of the settlement, in the local stock of legends.

Since the most distant times, the Pyrenees had the reputation of brimming over with precious metals. According to the Syrian chronicler Posidonius, the name they gave to the region denotes the Blazing Mountains. This refers to a conflagration that had once been started by shepherds. The whole range burned like an immense funeral pyre, and the rocks split open, releasing torrents of molten silver. After all the metal had solidified, the shepherds, not realising its value, allowed it to be taken away by the Phoenicians who loaded up a great number of ships with the precious metal. Also, having nothing to lose by it, they even made the silver into anchors. The fire lit by herdsmen, a strange legend adds, spread far to the north and ceased miraculously at Orval, to-day known as Paray-le-Monial, where the Celts found refuge and erected a "stone of witness" to the Virgin who bore the Holy Child.

Another legend, reported by Louis Fédié claims that, in the caves that used to connect with the subterranean passages of the castle of Rennes, there had always lived a race of troglodytes who were as ignorant of the passage of time as they were of the light of day. Besides recalling the memory of a prehistoric people, it is easy to recognise here the widespread tradition concerning mysterious beings that inhabit the mines, who either revealed the entrance to men or else denied them access, according to their whim.

In the same way, we could in passing acknowledge a divinity who is familiar in Gaulish mythology. She is the guardian of abandoned mines or the tutelary goddess of the beneficial waters, the grandmother of so many of our fairies and maidens, the White Queen, who plays so important a role in this region. For in the fabulous appearance of this queen there are combined many such historic memories, as we shall soon see. But for the time being, it is upon another group of traditions that we must fix our attention.

"The name of Rennes evokes above all a story of gold lying abandoned in hiding places from which, at the end of the nineteenth century, the local Curé recovered it."

These are the opening lines of the remarkable work, which the keeper of the library of Carcassonne, M. René Descadeillas, has recently dedicated to Rennes and its last Seigneurs. The author proceeds as follows:

Whoever hears this remark will immediately ask himself,

"What events in the distant past could have been the origin of such a situation? Through what chain of circumstances would anyone have been led to conceal treasure in this lonely and desolate spot?"

This last question mark sums up the entire historic enigma of Rennes and the whole secret held by Bérenger Saunière.

It would seem that at Rennes, as at Bethlehem, the first arrivals at the grotto were shepherds. Long before Saunière in fact, it was a shepherd who had the dangerous privilege of laying his hands upon the mysterious treasure. As if to make the anecdote even more fitting, the name of this shepherd was Paris.

Thus it was that in the spring of the year 1645 Ignace Paris, a young shepherd of Rennes, was searching for a lost sheep. Suddenly he heard it bleating. The animal had fallen to the bottom of a chasm. Paris climbed down to find a narrow passage, which plunged underground. He followed it and discovered, wonder-struck, a grotto wherein lay skeletons amongst piled-up heaps of gold.

He then filled his beret with pieces of the precious metal and hastened back to the village to recount his adventure, armed with this substantial evidence. But since he obstinately refused to reveal the exact place, no one believed him. He was accused of having simply committed a robbery and was therefore stoned to death. Told like this, the story strongly resembles a legend. However any similarities are only deceptive because the shepherd Paris did really exist and the ruins of his house can still be seen close to Rennes.

> Like a wretched and naked being,
> With his haggard visage
> And his hornèd and bald pate,
> And armed with a halberd,
> At the foot of this white mountain
> The angel of a mongrel race,
> Speaking low and wildly,
> Keeps perpetual guard
> Over this immense wealth
> That I can see from this rock,
> As if I had come
> To spy on him
> And steal the booty
> If he is not careful.

Filled with a droll and enigmatic charm, this little poem of

Labouisse-Rochefort illustrates a legend that he himself tells us in his *Voyage to Rennes-les-Bains* written in 1832.

At Blanchefort the devil guards a treasure of nineteen and a half millions to within a few sous. One fine day a local shepherdess saw the devil high up on the mountains displaying his gold pieces. She soon called the villagers to come and see this uncommon sight, but by the time they had arrived upon the scene the devil had again hidden his treasure and had disappeared. The villagers discussed the matter, and then went to Limoux to consult a breich[1], who, in exchange for an honest payment in advance and a promise that they would let him have one half of the gold, offered to try conclusions with the devil.

"But," said he to the peasants, "as soon as you hear cries, you must hasten to my assistance."

Having said this, the breich went to battle with the Evil One. The peasants soon heard loud noises and cries so horrible that they all took to their heels and fled. The breich returned, furious:

"Cowards, we have now lost everything and it's all your fault. I had already got a rope around his money bag, but you were not there to help me." Then, leaving the shame-faced peasants, he returned to Limoux.

It may be added that the Marquis de Fleury, Seigneur of Rennes and of Blanchefort, on whose lands this affair had

---

1. The langue d'oc word "breich" means "wizard".

taken place, brought an action against the villagers for
violation of his property. It is unfortunate that the
proceedings of this lawsuit have not been preserved, for
they could hardly have failed to be most picturesque. At
any rate it is possible to give an approximate date to the
legend, since it was only in 1767 that the Fleury family, of
whom we shall have much to say later, came to Rennes.

Without anticipating any of the comments relating to
these two narratives, we may point out that, unlike the
preceding events, they are not associated with the mining
folklore. The treasure of which they speak is not a gift of
nature; it is a hoard deposited by the hand of man. In one
case it is guarded by skeletons, in the other by the master
of Hades. The treasure is associated with chthonian
imagery: the gold of Rennes is the gold of the dead.

To the legends, which confirm the existence of a
treasure in the neighbourhood of Rennes, there may be
added various traditions relating to its origin and nature.

First, it has been said that Queen Blanche of Castille,
driven from Paris by the Shepherds' Crusade of 1214, came
to seek refuge in the Razès, she previously having caused
the Castle of Blanchefort to be built and concealed her
riches therein. The troubles died down and she returned
to the capital, having confided the secret of the hiding place
to her son Saint-Louis. The latter in his turn, passed it on to
his son, Philip the Bold, who was suddenly overtaken by
death before being able to inform his own son Philip the
Fair. Thus, the secret of the treasure of Blanchefort was lost.

According to another tradition, the castle of Blanchefort took its name from a visit paid by Blanche of France, the daughter of Saint-Louis, who had concealed a treasure in the neighbourhood.

These accounts are certainly attractive by reason of their odour of mystery, but be that as it may, history forbids us to believe them completely. Probably founded by the Visigoths, the castle of Blanchefort was, in the twelfth century, the prize stake in a very harsh struggle. The Benedictine Abbey of Alet aspired to seize it from its Seigneur Bernard de Blanchefort. Pope Calixtus II intervened in person in the legal battle, which he decided in 1119 in favour of the priests. Nevertheless, Bernard de Blanchefort then took up arms against them and after a struggle lasting eleven years, he forced the Pope to yield. In 1210 during the crusade against the Albigenses, Blanchefort was captured and destroyed by the French barons and was never rebuilt[1].

Thus neither Blanche of Castille, who was then only an adolescent and not yet queen, nor Blanche of France, who was not yet born, could have visited the place. In view of this we must give up the notion that this was the origin of Blanchefort's name. Between Blanchefort and these two White Queens, there exist no other links except those of a poetic analogy.

---

1. In 1238, the "men of Blanchefort" paid only one sou for their taxes. They were still, from the fiscal point of view, linked up with Coustaussa — by a promissory note of Pierre de Voisins according to a charter of Louis VIII. Since that time, then, there has been no castle, and not even a village.

But the legends are never of a White Queen alone. That of Rennes is concerned with three personages, the third has no treasure except a goblet: her melancholy memory still haunts the ruins of the castle of Peyrepertuse.

Guarding the ground of la Croix, in the Corbières this imposing fortress was erected by the Visigoths, then transformed in the eleventh century by the families of Bézalu and Fenouillède, descended from the Count of Razès Béra. Its ramparts shelter the statue of a woman, at which passers-by used to throw stones to ensure that she didn't bewitch them. According to the tradition, there were also, on the upper stories of the dungeon,

"Secret doors constructed from a single block like the tombs of the Kings of Judah. These doors consisted of a heavy stone turning on a pivot and let in flush with the wall."

Hence it was to a most isolated place that a queen of Castille named Blanche, having received news of serious trouble in her country, came to find refuge. Sad and in poor health, she spent her time in prayer and on lonely walks. One day, when she had gone to drink at the spring, which flowed at the foot of the ramparts, her silver goblet slipped from her hand and rolled down to the foot of the precipice. Some centuries later it was found once more by a shepherd and preserved as a treasure at Caudiès, in the Fenouillède, where it could be inspected until the coming of the Revolution.

Suffering from scrofula, this White Queen went one day to the waters of Rennes, and her illness disappeared immediately. This was an event so much more remarkable since only the King of France on the day of his anointing had the power to heal this disease by the simple laying on of hands. Now cured, the Queen tarried a while longer in the Razès, then, on the strength of false reports, she returned to her own country where her enemies caused her to be put to death.

But it is the most ancient of the traditions concerning the treasure of Rennes that is the most fascinating. Here it is, just as it was recorded by the Razès historian, Louis Fédié.

> The people of the Middle Ages believed that the precious metals extracted from the mine at Blanchefort did not originate in an enriched seam beneath the earth, but in a deposit of gold and silver ingots buried in the caves of the fortress by its original masters, the Visigothic Kings.

This tradition is very strange, since it goes against all the mediaeval beliefs concerning mines. To our ancestors, metals germinate and grow in the bosom of the earth, as do plants. In the sixteenth century, Bernard Palissy still shared this conviction and wrote,

"The Earth is never idle; what is naturally used up within her, she renews."

Mines, one might say, are like the fields. The more one works them the more fertile they become. This belief should not appear surprising because the processes of extraction are scarcely prolific and the earth's crust seemed to be inexhaustible. Taking into account such myths, the history of the gold hidden in an ancient mine would seem to be almost reasonable. It is also a history that is both poetic and astute. To disguise smelted gold as native gold is, one might say, a rather clever stratagem.

And what better hiding place for a treasure than a mine which has already been explored, exploited and worked out, where no one goes (unless it is someone who is party to the secret) since everybody knows that it is no longer possible to find any metal there?

Having reviewed these different traditions, it is now necessary for us to pass them across the sounding board of criticism and listen for any echoes, be they discordant or harmonious, of facts already well established by history.

First of all it must be emphasised that the gold of Rennes is not a myth. Catel, who was Councillor to the Parliament of Toulouse, in his *Memoirs of the History of Languedoc*, mentioned the existence of gold and silver mines near Rennes-les-Bains in 1633. A century later, in 1734, Lamoignon de Basville, steward of Languedoc wrote:

> The Romans had, in former times, gold mines in these mountains. Several openings cut in the rocks and extensive workings are to be seen there. But whether the mines became exhausted, or whether the art of locating them has been lost, the treasures, if there are any, are now so well hidden that no one troubles to search for them any more.

In 1775 in his monumental *Natural History of the Province of Languedoc,* Gensanne remarks in his turn:

> Near this place there has been considerable working of copper, lead and silver mines, particularly so among the mountains of Cardou and Roco Negro. But all these workings are now silted up, and it is only by the old debris that we have been able to distinguish the nature

of the mines that were worked there. It is much the same in the gold and silver mine, which we were told was exploited at the mountain of Blanchefort, a good quarter of a league below Rennes-les-Bains.

Finally in 1800 in his essay on *The Department of Aude*, addressed to the Minister of the Interior, the Prefect Barante drew attention to the following:

...two seams of silver, copper and lead in the mountains of Cardou and of Roco Negro to the north-east of Rennes-les-Bains in the direction of Montferrand...

...seams of gold and of silver eight or nine hundred fathoms to the south-east of the village of Rennes-les-Bains in the mountain of Blanchefort.

We have been able to verify these statements on the actual site. The seam of gold running from south to north and extending for about fifty metres is located within plots 625 and 626 of Section A of the cadastral survey. Formerly this seam commenced at ground level in plot 633. But it is necessary to emphasise strongly that if Catel is to be believed, all the mines in the region were worked out before the beginning of the seventeenth century. This would explain the failure of repeated attempts at exploitation from this period up to the commencement of the nineteenth century.

On the 24th August in the year 410, the Visigoth King Alaric the Old took possession of the city of Rome, which was then pillaged for six days, in the course of which enormous spoils were seized, including the plunder taken to Rome from the Temple of Jerusalem that the emperor Titus had sacked in the seventieth year of our era.

Solomon had allocated to the building of the original temple more than five hundred tons of gold and silver. In the sanctuary were deposited the ritual objects: Ark, Mercy Seat, Altar of Incense, Communion Table and seven-branched candlestick; all of which had been made according to the instructions given by Jehovah Himself; these together comprised a sacred treasure. Neither their metal, nor their weight, nor their form could be modified, and they remained immutable.

The temple also contained the product of tributes and offerings, which were received when the State was in danger. Later on, the temple was often pillaged but the more precious of its treasures were never seized because they were concealed in secure hiding places. Destroyed by Nebuchadnezzar but rebuilt by Esdras, then enlarged and beautified by Herod the Great and Herod Agrippa between A.D. 20 and A.D. 64, it had recovered all its splendour by the time that Titus captured Jerusalem. The Jewish historian Flavius Josephus compared it at that time to "a sun rising above the peak of a mountain of snow". Over its white defensive walls, the roof was roughcast with innumerable gold-covered needles, so that birds would not perch thereon.

Titus could not prevent his soldiers from setting fire to the building, but he took possession of its riches, the abundance of which may be estimated when we read that after he had allowed a portion to go into circulation, the gold market in Syria soon slumped. This fact will bring second thoughts to those who assert that the descriptions of the temple have been exaggerated by oriental emphasis even if they are not purely symbolic.

However, Titus sold only the ingots and the facing tiles. He transported the sacred objects to Rome. The finest are represented on his triumphal arch, such as the famous golden candlestick, which weighed a talent (thirty-four kilograms) and was carried by a slave. This treasure was installed in the Temple of Peace, then later in the Imperial Palace. According to the historian Procopius, Alaric invaded Rome in order to seize this trophy.

By its magnificence, the treasure of the Temple of Jerusalem fascinated all the chroniclers of antiquity. Many writings make it possible for us to follow step by step its vicissitudes up to the time of its capture by Alaric. After this, history becomes silent on the matter. This silence is most strange because if such famous jewels had much later been taken from the Visigoths, whether by the Franks or by the Arabs, then it is reasonable to suppose that the chroniclers would have recorded the matter.

The Frankish historian Frédégaire and the Arab chronicler El Macin both described in detail the treasure of the Visigothic kings. And they recount how it was captured at Toulouse by Clovis and then at Toledo by the Saracens, but they do not mention among the objects seized, anything which originated in the Temple of Jerusalem. Surely one must speculate whether the Visigoths,

being Christians who could not have failed to attach an
exceptional value to the treasures of the temple, did
not themselves manage to remove such precious objects
to an impregnable location, being well acquainted with
the avidity of conquerors.

In the fifth century when the Visigoths had become
masters of what later became Languedoc, their state
treasure was made up of two very distinct portions. One
portion comprised the tributes and personal jewels of the
kings who defrayed all public expenditure. This was stored at
Toulouse; on the other hand there was what was termed
the Ancient Treasure formed from the booty that the nation
had accumulated in the course of its conquering wanderings.
This sacred treasure was at one and the same time
the memorial of the ancestral exploits and a magical
guarantee of the power and continuity of the State, which
treasure the King himself could not touch, save only when
the very existence of the nation was in jeopardy.

In addition to the spoils from the Temple of Jerusalem,
this treasure included the Missorium, a massive golden plate
weighing five hundred pounds, which was placed on the
altar during Mass, and which Aetius had offered to King
Thorismond. Also there was the Emerald Table, a fabulous
ornament, the surface of which was no doubt of glass but
in this there were set three rows of pearls, the whole
being supported on sixty golden feet. During the reign
of Alaric II, this treasure was deposited at Carcassonne.
In A.D. 507 Clovis, having captured Toulouse and the
treasure that was located there, besieged Carcassonne,

which was saved only by the intervention of Theodoric, King of the Goths of Italy. In the course of the war, Alaric II was killed.

Alaric's son Amalaric being a minor, Theodoric took over the regency and, since Carcassonne was henceforward too exposed, removed the Ancient Treasure to Ravenna; but he returned it to Amalaric when the latter reached an age to govern.

In the seventh century, the Francs, extending their conquest, captured Narbonne, where they succeeded in securing only sixty chalices, fifteen patens and twenty collars. The Visigoths had in fact transported a part of the Ancient Treasure to the neighbourhood of Toledo, their Spanish capital. However, the Arabs reached there in A.D. 711, securing amongst the booty the famous Missorium. The remainder of the treasure, which comprised in particular nine massive votive gold crowns ornamented with sapphires, was discovered during the nineteenth century at Guarrazar near Toledo and was displayed in the museum of Cluny in Paris until 1943, the date when Pétain presented it to Franco. M. H.-P. Éydoux in his book *Light on Gaul* wrote,

"Can anyone find in France today a collection as brilliant and sumptuous as that of Guarrazar? This possibility cannot be excluded."

To the north of the Pyrenees, the Visigothic kingdom, at one time so formidable, soon became reduced to the Razès alone. Rhedae then became triply powerful. From the military point of view it was the key to communication with Spain and included two fortresses and four towers. From the religious point of view, there were two churches, St Marie and St John the Baptist, which was a monastery seeking to become a Bishop's palace. Finally its economic importance was by no means negligible. Rhedae comprised thirty thousand inhabitants and it included in one street alone fourteen butchers' shops.

Might that portion of the sacred treasure of the Visigoths, which neither the Francs nor the Arabs seem to have discovered, perhaps have been entrusted to the rugged land of the Razès?

It is understandable that some may have imagined that the gold of Solomon had thus been restored to the ore-bearing earth of the Pyrenees from whence perhaps it came and that, being returned to mother Earth, it had been infused with new life, germinating, growing and multiplying like wheat.

Certain facts however give a most peculiar twist to this dream. Shortly after the foundation of their order, the Templars installed themselves in the Razès, thanks to their links with two families of the district, both of them being well-to-do and turbulent, namely the Blancheforts and the A Niorts. Between 1132 and 1137 Arnaud, Bernard and Raimond de Blanchefort granted the Templars estates at Pieusse, Villarzel and Esperaza[1]. In 1147, they settled at Bézu and at Campagne-sur-Aude, on lands that had been ceded to them by the A Niort family.

---

1. *Cartulary of the Templars of Douzens.* Published by Pierre Gérard and Elisabeth Magnou under the direction of Philippe Wolff, Paris, 1965.

In 1156, the Order of the Temple elected a new Grand Master, who was none other than Bertrand de Blanchefort. It was at this time that the Templars of the Razès, through the mediation of their associates in the Rhineland, arranged that a colony of labourers should come from Germany and settle on the plateau of Lauzet between Blanchefort and Rennes. The soldier-monks subjected these workers to a military discipline, forbidding them, under pain of most severe sanctions, from mixing with what there was of a local population[1]. Only the very special character of the work on which they were engaged can explain this segregation. In fact they were working the gold mine of Blanchefort.

The famous Order who held the guardianship of the Temple of Jerusalem did not however extract much gold from this mine, which had already been exploited by the Romans. Furthermore (if one is to believe the engineer, César D'Arcons who, in the seventeenth century, was responsible for mining activities in the region) the Germans employed in the work were metal founders rather than miners. After that, one can better understand the most ancient tradition of the gold of Rennes according to which this gold did not come from a mine but from a deposit of Visigothic origin.

A hundred years after they had ceded Bézu and Campagne-sur-Aude to the Templars, we find the A Niort family in the same historical setting as one of the heroines

1. Communication from Abbé M.-R. Mazières.

of the legends woven around the gold of Rennes; Blanche of Castille.

This was at the time of the crusade against the Albigenses. Two generations of the Seigneurs of A Niort, who were ardently attached to the Cathar faith, rendered illustrious service under the banner of Toulouse against Simon de Montfort and Pierre de Voisins, his Seneschal for the Razès. Simon had richly endowed Pierre at the expense of Blanchefort and of A Niort and in 1215 gave him Rennes, Blanchefort and Campagne. But the A Niort family for their political ends made use of allies in the two camps so effectively that the Pope himself could not come to grips with them. It was only by approaching the Regent of France, Blanche of Castille, that in 1237 he was able to have them condemned as heretics by a tribunal on which was sitting Pierre de Voisins.

The likelihood of punishment by death or by perpetual imprisonment and the realisation that their property would be confiscated, finally persuaded the A Niort family to concede, so against all expectations they soon recovered their liberty and a portion of their estates.

In 1243, independent Occitania had nearly broken up, but the last Albi bastion, Montségur, still held out as if in defiance.

"The dragon's head must be cut off," said Blanche of Castille who in fact longed to take possession of the fortress with an unusual passion, which could hardly be explained by her Catholic zeal. Is it possible that Blanche had come to Occitania as the legend suggests?

We don't know, but it seems that, day by day, she followed events closely. In the autumn of 1243, after a five months siege, the situation of the defenders of Montségur had become desperate and it became necessary to consider negotiation, a hardly agreeable prospect since apparently they had little or no hope of obtaining mercy.

In fact Pierre-Roger de Mirepoix, the commandant, and many of the defenders had not only provided a safe haven for heretics, but during the previous year had massacred eleven inquisitors at Avignonet. Furthermore the Count of Toulouse, Raimond VII, whose latest attempt at insurrection had just come to grief, sought to make his peace with the Pope and reluctantly undertook to surrender Montségur.

At this moment, a man appeared who was going to be embroiled in some mysterious negotiations: Ramon d'A Niort. Being the son-in-law of Pierre-Roger de Mirepoix and the brother-in-law of the Seigneur of Montségur, Ramon de Perelha, he had the ear of Raimond VII, and without doubt it was Blanche of Castille who had granted him pardon in the preceding year.

At Christmas 1243 he sent an emissary named Escot de Belcaire to Montségur. The emissary, after having ingratiated himself with the besiegers, gained access to the castle, where he delivered certain letters to Pierre-Roger and informed him that a signal-fire would be lit on the nearby mountain of Bidorta,

"...if the Count of Toulouse managed his affairs with circumspection."

The emissary then departed and on the following night

the summit was in fact lit up. Some days later two heretics, Mattheus and Pierre Bonnet, succeeded in getting out of the castle laden with "gold, silver and a great amount of money", which for the time being they concealed in a converted grotto.

This affair, wrote M. Fernand Niel, brings to the scene two characters whose behaviour, in the light of the circumstances, must warrant some consideration — the Count of Toulouse and Ramon d'A Niort. The defenders of Montségur would doubtless have disapproved of the sending of a messenger merely to point out that the Count of Toulouse should manage his affairs better, had not this been related to the fate of the garrison. On the other hand it is hard to imagine Escot de Belcaire climbing up Bidorta and lighting beacon-fires on its peak simply to confirm what he had come to say two days previously.

The most logical reason for his mission would therefore be related to the secret transactions being carried out between Pierre-Roger de Mirepoix and some other person outside, but who could this other person have been?

On the first day of March 1244, the Montségur defenders declared themselves ready to negotiate. The conditions that they were granted seem most unexpected. Not only were they permitted to retire with their arms, equipment, and the honours of war (with the exception of the heretics, who refusing to recant, were committed to the notorious blazing stake) but also they were even absolved of the murder of the inquisitors. Finally they were granted the right to remain in the castle for a further two weeks. On 13th March, during the night before the actual surrender, the three Albigenses, Hugo, Poitevin and Amiel Aicard, having been lowered by ropes, slipped out of the castle down the rock face using footholds that had been hewn out with a pick.

"And this was accomplished so that the church of the heretics should not lose its treasure, which was hidden in the forests — and the fugitives knew the hiding place[1]."

By allowing these three men to escape, Pierre-Roger de Mirepoix violated the clause of the surrender, which obliged him to return to the church the obdurate heretics. He therefore took the risk of exposing to certain death all those, including himself, who had managed to secure a safe and free existence, of which they could otherwise have had little hope.

What was it then, (still insists M. Niel) about this treasure that it must be saved at any price? We might be content to believe that the fugitives were not rescuing any material treasure. Had not this treasure already been moved out two months earlier by Mattheus and Pierre Bonnet? This time, we believe, it concerns even more precious objects of a spiritual treasure, possibly parchments on which were written the secrets of a religion, which preserved its adepts from fearing death at the stake.

---

1. Evidence of Arnaud-Roger de Mirepoix in *Doat*, Vol. XXII, p.129.

However, another theory has been advanced. Blanche of Castille could only have obtained the surrender of Montségur by the exchange of highly important genealogical documents that the defenders of the castle, once they had them in their possession, would have concealed in a safe place. Were these then the letters handed over by Ramon d'A Niort's messenger?

Was it this that was carried by those who escaped on that last night? Finally, was it this that, as some people assume today, had been recovered much later, and 'hidden under a bushel'? It is doubtful whether we shall ever know. The surrender of Montségur preserves its mystery since the defenders are no longer in a position to explain why they were so hard to please, nor their adversaries to tell us why they made a present without gaining anything in return.

Pierre Roger de Mirepoix ended his days a free man. Pierre de Voisins, in 1244 was compelled to hand over Campagne to the Templars. In 1247 he had also to give up several estates to Ramon d'A Niort since Louis IX had received this equivocal character into his court and had taken notice of his requests, as one does when dealing with someone who needs careful handling.

In 1269 Blanche of France, the daughter of Louis IX, married the heir to the throne of Castille, Ferdinand, dubbed Prince of la Cerda, that is to say Son of the Sow, because he had on his shoulder a tuft of hair like the bristles of a pig. Six years later Ferdinand died prior to his father's death, leaving two sons, Alphonse and Ferdinand. Sanche, the younger brother of the dead prince, took possession of the two children, arranged for himself to be proclaimed king and then exiled his sister-in-law Blanche. The latter crossed over the mountains and in 1280 settled in the Razès, not however, as the legend suggests at Blanchefort that had by then been destroyed, but at Rennes where she resided with Paul de Voisins, Seigneur of the domain.

She brought substantial funds with her with which to pay the army that she had decided to raise so as to liberate and re-establish as king the young Alphonse, who was henceforward known as El Desdichado, the disinherited one.

This scheme ensured a three-fold support; namely that of her brother, the King of France, Philippe III the Bold, that of King Jacques I of Majorca and that of the Templars. In fact Jacques I of Majorca had recently entered into conflict with his brother Pierre III of Aragon. Beyond the Pyrenees there were therefore two parties, the Aragonese and the Majorcan. The King of France and the Templars supported the latter, the first in order to counter the traditional Aragonese demands upon Languedoc and the others because the Kingdom of Majorca was their creation and their territory. Moreover, the King of Aragon had just made them submit to a series of political humiliations. In 1280 a meeting of the three kings took place at Toulouse. Pierre III agreed to snatch the Princes of Cerda away from Sanche, but he did this in order to secure them himself and therefore claimed that he would only return the Princes to their mother in exchange for the Carcassonne district and the Razès.

At the same time, amid the intrigues of which the Princes were the object, there was played a decisive phase of Spanish unification. In fact King Alphonse X, the grandfather of the Disinherited One, proposed to split up his estates so as to offer the kingdom of Jaen to his grandson. However, the Cortès, being opposed to this division, deposed him and accordingly he appealed to the Sultan of Morocco. Sanche however, then repulsed the Sultan, so appearing as the champion of national independence. Sanche was accordingly proclaimed King in 1284.

It became evident that his share had grown too large. After years of bargaining, El Desdichado ended by renouncing his rights in exchange for a sum of five hundred thousand maravedis[1] of gold, which were to be paid in annual instalments. But one of these precious convoys never reached him. It had been attacked on the journey. Public rumour attributed the robbery to Paul de Voisins, Seigneur of Rennes, who was forced to absent himself for some time. El Desdichado settled in Languedoc where he became Seigneur of Lunel[2] and there founded a family.

In August 1283, Philippe III the Bold paid a discreet visit to the Razès, accompanied by his son, the future Philippe the Fair then fifteen years of age. Where actually did the King and the Crown Prince go? First they went to the

---

1. Translation note: Maravedi — Spanish currency value in 1913 equivalent to one and a half centimes.
2. Lunel is the only town in France founded by Jews who were established before the Roman conquest, and an ancient synagogue may be seen there. Its coat of arms bears a crescent moon from which the inhabitants derive the name "Moon Fishers".

Templars at Campagne-sur-Aude, then to Brenac to visit the A Niort family. In the course of his stay, Prince Philippe, whose manner reputedly had a certain frigidity, struck up a warm friendship with the two young A Niort Seigneurs, Ramon and Udaut[1].

It was the evidence concerning this journey that gave rise to the legend according to which Philippe III would have learned from his father about the secret of Rennes. He would have been about to collect the final details of the location when he died without having been able to pass the secret over to Philippe the Fair.

In 1285 Philippe the Bold died and Philippe the Fair ascended the throne. His young friend Udaut d'A Niort soon became a Templar at Campagne.

On Friday 13th October 1307 all the Templars in the Kingdom of France were arrested. A drama commenced in which, as every schoolboy knows, the principal actors were King Philippe the Fair, the Grand Master Jacques de Molay and Pope Clement V, whose real name was Bertrand de Goth. What was not so well known was that it was the same Bertrand de Goth who, through the lineage of his mother, Ida de Blanchefort, was the grand-nephew of Bertrand de Blanchefort, the Grand Master of the Temple, who a century and a half previously had brought about the working of the mines in his native earth by the famous German metal-founders. Another fact worthy of notice is that not one of the Templars of Bézu was arrested.

---

1. Archives of Abbé M.-R. Mazières.

In 1310 Philippe the Fair sent his chamberlain, the noted Enguerrand de Marigny, to the Razès with the object of taking over all the assets belonging to the Templars.

On the whole, he succeeded in this, but it is very strange that he could not seize anything from the Templars of Bézu. Five years later Marigny was well and truly hanged at the conclusion of a dubious trial. In 1319, thirteen of the Templars of Roussillon disappeared mysteriously, one after the other. Perhaps the Templars of Bézu had been able to prove that they were not the possessors but only the trustees of assets, which had been deposited within their territory. Perhaps this very argument had been put forward by the depositors themselves. Perhaps even, the agents of the royal power did not find anything because the treasure had been concealed in a very safe hiding place indeed. It must not be forgotten that while they were at Bézu, the Templars were actually on the lands of the Voisins. Did the latter consider providing a safe haven on their own account for the riches that were threatened with seizure? This would appear very reasonable in the light of the events that began to take place at Bézu some thirty years later.

In 1340 the agents of the royal Seneschal arrived at the Château of Bézu in order to arrest two knights, Guilhem Catala and Pierre de Palajan of Coustaussa. These persons were in fact convicted of having "on several occasions at Bézu and elsewhere melted and struck false money" with the complicity of two women Agnès Mayssène of Caderone and Brunissende of Gureyo. Caught in the act, the culprits knew just what to do: they sent back home as their own emissary, one of those who had come to unmask them, Guilhem Servin. Little is known of Pierre de Palajan or of Agnès Mayssène, but on the other hand Guilhem Catala was certainly no ordinary person. He was in fact the nephew of Jacques Fournier, otherwise known as the reigning Pope Benedict XII. And he was also the son-in-law of the Seigneur of Rennes, Jacques de Voisin whose wife was none other than Brunissende de Gureyo. The culprits obtained their pardon four years later.

To coin false money could at that period have meant two distinct activities. It either signified putting into circulation coins made from inferior alloy, being poorer in precious metal than required by law, or else making and circulating coins of good alloy but without having the legal right so to do. Now at the time when this affair took place no one had the right to coin money, "...save by authorisation of the Pope or of some other sovereign."

The Voisins owed their advancement to Montfort. So, did they coin and circulate the false money with the assent of the King of France Philippe VI de Valois, who then supported the claims of Jean de Montfort to the throne of Brittany in opposition to the English? This would seem doubtful, since then they would not have been pursued by the agents of the central power. Did Guilhem Catala do the same thing with the blessing of the Pope his uncle? It is possible that from that period onwards the Holy See became interested in the gold of Rennes.

But, be that as it may, in order to coin money, one must have metal. Whence came the gold that the Voisins transformed into chinking coins? And why did they take such great risks instead of selling the metal just as it was?

It surely was because, for one reason or another, the provision and working of the metal could not be divulged. In other words the coining of the false money of Bézu made it possible to solve the problem which faced Bérenger Saunière many years later. How can one negotiate a treasure without also revealing its existence? To this problem there is but one solution, which is to smelt the metal, producing what could be passed as legal tender.

In 1352 the young King of Aragon and of Castille, Pierre I, who was before long dubbed The Cruel, married Blanche de Bourbon, sister-in-law of the Dauphin of France, the future Charles V. His mother had forced this political marriage when the young man was strongly attached to the beautiful Jeanne de Castro. Unlike many others, Pierre would not resign himself to the nuptial bargain, even on the surface. Scarcely three days after the marriage he caused Blanche to be consigned to a convent at Medina, after which despite all remonstrance he continued to live without making any secret about the mate he had chosen.

Taking his misconduct as a pretext, the queen mother then stirred up his two brothers, Sanche and Henri de Trastamare, against him. But the plot failed and in 1361 Trastamare fled to France accompanied by his terrible Aragonese mercenaries and laid siege to Rennes-le-Château. The lower town was no longer in existence; the Aragonese had already destroyed it two hundred years earlier in the course of a raid.

But the Voisins had rebuilt the fortifications of the upper town, since it had by then become the chief town of their important domains. The mercenaries pillaged the monastery and then their artillery bombarded a tower wherein the powder magazine had been installed. The explosion opened up a breach in the ramparts through which they swarmed. Once within the walls, the invaders set about demolishing the church of Saint John the Baptist stone by stone. According to tradition, they were searching for a precious deposit. It is further said that the church was really a trap and that a rocking block of masonry precipitated fifteen of the over-curious assailants into an underground cavern, their bones being crushed. Finally came the sacking, the destruction and the massacre, which brought about a plague. From that day the once opulent Rennes has been nothing more than a village.

In order to silence the murmurs, Pierre The Cruel claimed that his wife had deceived him with his own brother Frederic[1]. Pierre then caused his brother to be executed. As regards the wretched Blanche, she died in 1362, having been assassinated in prison. It is not known whether she perished by poisoning, or by being stifled under her pillow like Desdemona.

However, the Pope and the King of France supported Trastamare's claims to the throne of Castille. The pretender crossed the mountains with his mercenaries,

---

1. Blanche could have had a son by Frederic, named Don Enrique, the founder of the Enriquez family. He was in fact reputed to have been related to the house of Castille without it being known in exactly what manner.

helped by Du Guesclin, who for this campaign, had recruited a number of western Seigneurs whose Albigensian families had been ruined by reason of the crusade. Pierre took flight and Trastamare was proclaimed King. His victory was however only ephemeral; supported by the English under the Black Prince, Pierre defeated his adversary and once again Trastamare took refuge in France. But his mercenaries had left there such memories that he received only a frigid welcome. All that he was able to secure from the King was sanctuary in the castle of Peyrepertuse, where he lived for several years with his wife Jeanne de Penafiel and their children.

Hence, the melancholy queen of Castille who came to Peyrepertuse was not named Blanche but Jeanne.

"To weep like Diana at the edge of these fountains; her love being lonely and ever threatened by danger."

Thus as is often the case, popular memory has attributed to one individual, several persons who were involved at the same place, or in the same events. This has willingly lent to Jeanne de Trastamare the name and the touching misfortunes of Blanche de Bourbon and no doubt also those of Blanche of France.

But history seems here to take a malignant pleasure in meddling with myth. Those knights of Albigensian origin who accompanied Du Guesclin into Castille were called the Moundis, that is to say the Pure Ones. To the people they were the White Gentlemen and to their enemies the White Company, since they bore on their jerkins the white Cross which much later became the badge of the Armagnac party. Eventually it was near the Aragon frontier in a White Castle, the exact location of which is not known, that Du Guesclin rejoined Trastamare.

"It was King Henry within the castle white who claimed his heritage by royal right."

In terms of this journey into history, into legend and into their mutual relationship, one may venture to suggest the following as being probable:

1. Since the Middle Ages a tradition has existed according to which a treasure (or several treasures) has been hidden in the neighbourhood of Rennes.

2. This tradition is not absurd since it is supported by certain well-established facts and by certain probabilities. The presence (probable) of a Visigothic treasure at Carcassonne. The existence of a gold mine at Blanchefort. The exploitation of this mine during the Middle Ages. The deposit (probable) of funds of the Majorcan party. The coining of false money at Bézu. The discovery in the nineteenth century of important amounts of melted down gold.

3. Nevertheless no document, both ancient and authenticated, exists which would permit us to confirm these theories as being certainties.

If we now consider this tradition in its mythical aspects, its theme becomes richer as it is developed.

The gold of Rennes is presented to us as a priceless hoard, of mysterious origin, which has played (or is destined to play) a very important political role in association with some particular community, church, state, religious order

or party. This gold most often appears to be connected
with the theme of plundering; the Albigensian church, the
ruling families such as A Niort, Blanche de Bourbon, the
Templars, and El Desdichado. In every case it concerns folk
of high rank whose legitimate rights have been violated,
whether rights of heritage or rights of blood.

On the other hand, the various versions of the tradition,
though historically in contradiction, share a convergent
mythology.

It is of little significance from the thematic point of view
whether the treasure is attributed to Blanche of Castille,
mother of Louis IX or to Blanche of Bourbon, Queen of
Castille; or whether it is located at Blanchefort rather than
at Bézu. In fact the ancient name of Bézu was Albedunum,
the true translation of which is Rochefort. So the treasure,
most poetically, shares the ubiquity of "Château Blanc"
which is its guardian.

Just as the analysis of a dream often appears as the name
of a place hidden behind that of a person, so Blanche de
Castille may well be a simple metaphor of Castillo Blanco
or of Château Blanc. After all, at Bézu just as at Blanchefort,
the treasure belongs to the "Whites": to the Albigenses,
to the White Cloaks or to the White Queens. Then,
as if to emphasise this whiteness, the legend, cleverly
employing sequences of events, causes it to stand out from
the dark background. So Blanchefort is opposed to Roco
Negro, the upper part of Rennes to the lower, the white
King to the black and the Devil to the Shepherdess.

This bipolar nature recalls to Baucent, according to the

vagaries of reflection and reverie, the enigmatic black and white standard of the Templars that is so reminiscent of the chessboard, which is both battlefield and the format for an abstract puzzle. Again, it reminds us of a mummer's mask, which is simultaneously a game and a disguise. In short, it symbolises the indissoluble unity of opposites, that of clear intellect and of nocturnal imagination. It is thus by its dialectic charm that the legend exerts its attraction.

The gold of Rennes is still by reason of its origin the gold of the dead; gold of the Visigothic kings who were buried with their treasure; gold of the Albigenses whom the Templars committed to the stake; gold of the queens, long dead in their dungeons; gold guarded by the master of hell or by skeletons.

Yet this gold has never been seen except by young shepherds, symbols of innocence. This last aspect of the legendary theme is not the least relevant, since it works on people's imagination as if to transmute hidden gold into some spiritual treasure.

In this respect, Bérenger Saunière was the exception. Certainly he was a pastor, but too soon he had lost the spirit of childhood and already felt presentiments of his own mortality. He could not prevent himself from acknowledging the whiff of brimstone in it all and when he had discovered the gold, he experienced the relentless conscience of a miscreant faced with the inscription on a tomb that recalled something of the innocence of Arcadia.

But we have not completely finished with the mythology of Rennes. It is under this heading that we shall mention (since we are unable to dispel the uncertainties about their source and intention) two very singular works published at Geneva in recent years in a very small number of copies. In both of these, the authors concealed their true identities under pseudonyms that were obviously symbolic.

The first one appeared in 1956 with the signature of Henri Lobineau and was entitled *Genealogy of the Merovingian Kings and Origins of Various French and Foreign Families of Merovingian Stock*, from Abbé Pichon, Dr. Hervé and The Parchments of Abbé Saunière of Rennes-le-Château (Aude).

The second appeared in 1963 being entitled *The Merovingian Descendants or The Riddle of Visigothic Razès*, written by Madeleine Blancasall and translated from the German by Walter Celse-Nazaire.

The theory outlined in these two works is, to say the least, surprising. According to the authors, the ancestral line of the last Merovingian King, Saint Dagobert II did not become extinct when he was assassinated in the forest of Woëvre near Stenay on the 23rd December 679. In fact, his son Sigebert IV (who most historians consider as having been assassinated at the same time as his father) took refuge at Rhedae, assumed the title of Count of Razès and founded a family. He died in 758 and was interred within the church, under the memorial stone known as the Chevalier.

It was this Sigebert IV who caused to be carved on the menhir of Cap de l'Hom, the stone figure near Rennes, the image of his father. In fact, this was sometimes represented in the region as that of Saint Dagobert.

Nothing is as obscure and little known as the history of the last Merovingians. Like their phenomenal origin, the disappearance of the kings of the first dynasty remains surrounded by mystery. This was the period of sensational events; murders, rapes, the substitution of babies, kings proclaimed and deposed only to reappear abruptly, and unfathomable genealogies.

Experts have recently thrown some light upon the relations that existed in this epoch, between the Rhine-Meuse area, which was the point of departure for the Merovingian flight on the one hand, and the district of Aude on the other. These relationships have been illustrated by the simultaneous discovery, in Merovingian cemeteries situated in Lorraine and near Castelnaudary, of skulls that have been ritually pierced. Toponomy already pointed to this possibility, since in the Aude district, Issel and la Sals corresponds to the Issel and the Sala of the Guelderland, whence the Salien Francs set forth.

Whatever its nature, the multiform treasure of Rennes has, thanks to modern and confidential authors, been enriched by a new aspect. It is not only the hidden treasure but also the hidden blood-line that has become a dynastic treasure and re-kindles a myth whose political rôle at various moments in our national history is far from being negligible; it is the myth of the Lost King.

ooOOoo

Since the fifteenth century the Razès seems to have lost all memory of its adventurous past. This is scarcely better reflected in the foggy mirror of tradition. The very earth spreads little by little a thick mantle of undergrowth over its ancient secrets. However, throughout this land there remain alliances, intrigues and envy. Even today such forces are still at work.

The house of Hautpoul was one of the most ancient and illustrious of the Languedoc region. Its founders were named the Kings of the Black Mountain, since this was their cradle and they owned the nearby gold mine of Salsines amongst others. The Hautpouls are to be found in the Crusades and then in the Albigensian war in the southern camp. In 1422 they allied their family with the Voisins, Seigneurs of Rennes, and it was in 1732 that François d'Hautpoul married Marie de Negri d'Ables, whose mysterious tombstone has already been mentioned.

But the trees, even when they are genealogical, do not completely hide the forest. From this tedious genealogy let us simply bear this in mind; from the fifteenth century onward, all the lands where have occurred these strange events that we have discussed, succeeded in regrouping under a single governor. From the Voisins the lands passed to Hautpoul-Blanchefort, thence to Fleury; three names which finish by becoming only one.

In 1644 François-Pierre d'Hautpoul, Baron of Rennes, had made his will and had then unified all those archives, which since the eleventh century had legalised the transmission of the fiefs and titles which he held.

The whole transaction had been registered on the 23rd November with Maître Captier, a notary of Esperaza. But after the death of the Baron d'Hautpoul, his heirs could not obtain any knowledge regarding either the will or the other documents: everything had mysteriously disappeared.

This period is also that during which the royal power was showing renewed interest in the mines of Razès. The Steward of Basville writes:

> M. Colbert formed a company in 1692 to deal with the working of these mines. He even brought in Swedish workmen for this project, but his good offices have only served to discover a few seams of copper which disappeared after a little time of working and which will not even pay for the cost of the discovery.

In 1695 the grandson of François-Pierre, by name Henri d'Hautpoul, Baron of Rennes died leaving four sons, Blaise, Charles, François and Joseph. He also left his will. Yet, contrary to the right of seniority, which then had the force of law, it was François who, although he was only the third eldest son, installed himself in the Castle of Rennes as master to manage the family estates. At the same time François assumed, as we have noted, the unusual title of Marquis of Blanchefort. What was even better, he became the guardian and possessor of the paternal testament that he refused to show to anyone for forty-eight years. To this collection of anomalies there is one other that is even more surprising; nobody in the family raised a voice in protest at his singular behaviour.

One hundred and thirty years after its mysterious disappearance, the will of François-Pierre d'Hautpoul again came to light in 1780 no less strangely, through another notary of Esperaza, Jean-Baptiste Siau. Learning of this, Pierre d'Hautpoul Seigneur of Serres, quite naturally demanded access to it. However, he received this surprising response from the notary,

"It would not be prudent on my part to give up possession of a testament of such great consequence." Then the documents again disappeared.

"What has become of these papers?" asks M. Descadeillas in his work *Rennes and its last Seigneurs.*

In vain would they be sought today, as they have been incorporated in legal contracts and have therefore never figured in the archives of the notary who held them. However, they would deliver us from the uncertainty that has long surrounded so many details of the genealogy of the Hautpoul[1] family.

In fact, in December 1780, the notary Siau had given over the famous papers to Marie de Negri d'Ables, widow of François d'Hautpoul-Blanchefort. Then in January 1781, the contents were confided to Abbé Antoine Bigou, Curé of Rennes-le-Château, who was also her chaplain. When Marie de Negri d'Ables reached the end of her life the normal procedure would have been for the family papers to be passed over to her eldest daughter Marie so that

---

1.René Descadeillas further remarks, "The contract referred to here is probably the judgement of confirmation in possession made 4th January 1664 by the steward of Bezons."

they would then be held by the Hautpoul-Félines family[1]. However the papers (or at any rate some of them) remained in the keeping of Elizabeth, the youngest surviving daughter.

Harassed by demands and even by threats of legal action from her sisters and brothers-in-law, she refused until her death to communicate all that she was holding. She stressed the fact that it would be necessary "to decipher and to distinguish between what was the property of the family and what was not theirs at all". She further pretended that she was unable to open her chests for fear that some precious pieces might go astray.

We shall not discus further how to explain why the title of Blanchefort passed, not to Marie who was the eldest daughter of François d'Hautpoul and who had married her cousin Hautpoul-Félines, but to the youngest of her sisters, Gabrielle. And indeed she was supported in this by the influence of her husband Paul-François-Vincent de Fleury.

By this marriage, the latter had inherited the mines of Roco Negro and of Cardou, near Rennes. However a certain Dubosc arrived at Rennes from Rouen in 1782 who, without seeking the least authorisation from the Marquis de Fleury, started to reopen the mines. When Fleury protested, Dubosc (who already was concessionaire for other mines in the district) declared that he was acting in accordance with an order of the King who had granted him the mining rights.

---

1. In March 1781, the famous Judge of Arms, Hughes d'Hozier de Sérigny had demanded from Antoine Bigou that he be allowed to read these papers so as to establish a contract, duly delivered 30th April 1781.

In fact his claim was supported by the Steward of Languedoc. Once more there was litigation. The Marquis de Fleury ended by getting the best of things and secured the mining concession on his own account, but by then it was 1789.

So many wills spirited away; such mysteries and lawsuits make one think that there was in fact some secret "of great consequence" held within the Hautpoul family. Was this the secret of a precious deposit, or perhaps that of ancestry that could not be revealed? Or even a combination of both these suggestions? In any case if there was a secret, its last legitimate holders could only have been Marie de Negri d'Ables, her daughter Elizabeth and their Chaplain, Antoine Bigou.

Marie de Negri d'Ables, Dame of Hautpoul de Blanchefort died at her castle at Rennes, aged 67 years, on 17th January 1781, at least if we are to believe her epitaph. This epitaph was drawn up by Abbé Antoine Bigou with as much care in its composition as that which Bérenger Saunière employed one hundred years later in its effacement. When one considers that Bigou spent two years on the task, one becomes surprised to read this strange text, lacking any apparent sense, where each line contains some fault or anomaly and where even the names of so illustrious a lady have twice been scraped away.

In August 1792, Abbé Bigou refused to take an oath of loyalty to the Republic. In September of the same year he emigrated secretly to Sabadell in Spain, at the same time as Mgr. de la Cropte de Chanterac who was the Bishop of Alet, Abbé Cauneilles the Curé of Rennes-les-Bains and other Priests. He died two years later.

The Marquis de Fleury also followed the road to exile. We can conjecture that it was he who, before his departure caused another stone to be carved, which was discovered only by chance much later. It had been buried under an ilex oak tree. It was lost again, to be re-discovered in 1928. This time it had been hidden in a hollow of rock on the mountain of Coumesourde, near Rennes-les-Bains. This also is a strange tombstone, as shown overleaf in Fig. 4.

"Where History has become silent, the stones still speak." says a proverb very dear to archaeologists. At Rennes, the stones were speaking with hidden words. One has to believe that they were even saying too much about the affair for the liking of some people, since there were those who tried to have them silenced and who still persist in trying to render them silent for ever; both the stones and those persons who have been able to glean the secrets they conceal.

ooOOoo

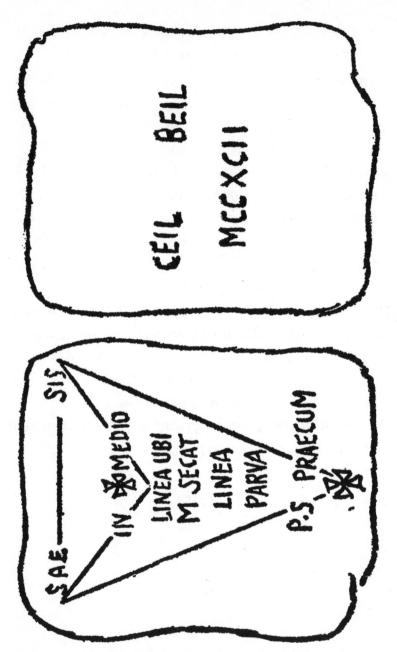

Fig. 4. The Coumesourde Stone.
(Illustration by Ernest Gros).

PART THREE

THE BARBERS OF MIDAS

Concerning reading, proper understanding in volves penetrating the meaning of the words to the deepest roots of etymology and language. This then, is the first principle of the art of reading. The second principle concerns memory. It is necessary to link the meanings that have been discovered, into a logical structure, without ever allowing any relevant details to become lost in the process.

Dominique Aubier. *Don Quixote, Prophet of Israel*.

Language provides the opportunity for unveiling secrets; that sphere of experience where truth reveals itself and explains itself.

Michel Foucault. *Words and Things*.

Discoveries of importance always profoundly modify the mental outlook of those who make them. Especially, the maker of a stupendous discovery would, if he were unable to reveal it, be the prisoner of an almost intolerable contradiction between his pride that would impel him to make it public and his fear, which would constrain him to remain silent. One can imagine him as being obsessed throughout his life by what he has seen, which was perhaps terrifying, but which cannot be disclosed to anyone.

Since early times a fable has existed which will make us realise the situation. It is that of the barber of Midas, who discovered that his master concealed under his cap the ears of an ass. He therefore whispered his secret to the earth after having dug a hole, which he then hastened to fill. But soon rushes sprang up there that, at the slightest breath of wind, spread abroad his indiscretion.

For such a man the only way out would be to speak while taking care not to be understood, or to be understood while ensuring that certain aspects are never overtly mentioned. But to achieve this, common language will be of little use. It will therefore be necessary for him to devise another sort of language; to create a sea into which can be cast without too much risk the message that has been placed within the bottle; that is to say, though he might not realise it, to re-invent the Hermetic art.

Successive custodians of the secret of Rennes might well have made this remarkable mental leap, so that they were inspired through the centuries to construct a wonderful puzzle. In this context, one might think that the celebrated saying of André Breton:

"The imaginary is something that tends to become true",
is nothing more than a rather timid turn of phrase.

This was at any rate the first idea that came to me on
that day in Paris during February 1964 when, after much
beating about the bush, two documents were entrusted to
me that I would swear put me on the trail of the most
unusual affair ever encountered.

These were the copies of two of the parchments that
Bérenger Saunière found beneath the high altar of his church.
On them one may read two passages written in Latin, from
the Gospels. The first, taken from John 12:1–12 is that
relating to the visit of Christ to Bethany where lived Lazarus,
Martha and Mary Magdalene (Fig.5; Manuscript I). The
second contains the parable of the ears of corn picked on
the Sabbath day (Fig.6; Manuscript II). Here it may be
observed that the writer has complicated the task because
he has combined in one single text the three versions of
the episode as contained in Luke 6:1–5, Matthew 12: 1–8
and Mark 2: 23–28.

Right from the start two important features about these
manuscripts struck me. In the first place, in spite of their
archaic style, these documents did not appear to be very
ancient. Furthermore, both of them seemed to constitute
ciphers. In the plain text of the first document, one
hundred and twenty eight supplementary letters have
been inserted, the sequence of which does not appear to
convey any specific meaning. In the second parchment can

be seen out-of-phase letters, other letters indicated by a dot, lines of varying lengths, etc. Finally, in both of these parchments there appear certain hieroglyphic marks that could be the keys by means of which the message can be read.

When confronted with documents such as these, one must be extremely wary. I have no particular competence either in ancient writings or in secret writings. My first step therefore, was to have the manuscripts submitted to palaeographic and cryptographic appraisement.

I first had a discussion with M. Debant, Diploma of the School of Palaeography and Director of the Departmental Archives for the Aude, and he willingly agreed to submit his conclusions in writing.

The following was the result:

1. That these documents were not in fact very ancient.

2. That they had been written by the same hand.

3. That their author had been instructed in mediaeval palaeography and epigraphy.

4. That he had put his skill to good use; not to commit a forgery that could not have deceived the specialists, but rather to draw the attention of the reader by means of intentional anomalies.

Later in the course of an interview, M. Debant told me that the documents could not be dated with any precision, but it seemed certain that they could not have been produced prior to the Renaissance.

✵

JESVSEVRGOANTCESEXATPESPASCSHAEVENJTTbETh9ANTAMVRAT
FVERAOTIAZA•VVSMORTVVVS9VEMMSVSCTYTAVITIYESVSFEACERVNT
LAVIEM•TTCAENAPMTbTETOMARThAhMINISTRRAbATLbASARVSO
YEROVNXVSERATTE•ATSCOVMLENTATLVSCVJMMARTALERGOACbCEP
TILKTbRAMYNNGENTTJNARATPFTSTTCT9PRETTOVSTETVNEXTTPE
APESTERVAETEXTEJRSTTCAYPTIRTSNSVTSPEPAESERTPTETAOMbESTM
YLFTTAESTEEXVNGETNTTOAAEREATXALTERGOVRNVMEXAGTSCTPVhL
TSETVTXTVAAXSCARJORTTS9V.IYERATCVhMTRAATTTVRVS9TVARECOSCVN
bEN VTVMNONXVENYTTGRECENPATSAENAARVSETAAATVMESGTE
GENTES?ATXTNVFEMhOECNON9VSTAAEEGAENTSPERRTINEbEAT
AACVTMSEA9VhMFVRELRTETLOVCVIOShCAhENSECA9VAEMVTTTEbA
NMTVRPOTRAbETEATXTTEJRGOTEShVSSTNEPTLLAMVNTTXAIEMS
EPVLGTVRAEMSEAESERVNETILL9VAPAVPJERESENhTMSEMPGERhA
bEMTTSNObLTTSCVMFMEAVTETMNONSESMPERhAVbEIISCJOGNO
VILTEROTZVRbAMV9LTAEXTMVAACTST9VTATLOLTCESTXETVENE
ARVNTNONNPROTEPRTESVm ETANTvM MSEAVILVZARVMPVTAER
ChmT9VEMKSVSCTAOVTTAMORRTVTSCPOGTTAVKERVNTAhVTEMP
RVTNCTPEJSSACEHCAOTVMVMTETLAZCARVMTNATERFTCTRENT9
LVTAMVLVTTPROP9TERTLhXVMAbThGNTCXVGTAAETSNETCRCA
AEbANTTNTESVM

NΘ IS

JÉSV. MEDELA. VVLNERVM ✛ SPES.VNA. POENITENTIVM.
PER. MAGDALANÆ. LACHRYMAS ✛ PECCATA. NOSTRA. DILVAS.

✵

Fig. 5. Manuscript I.

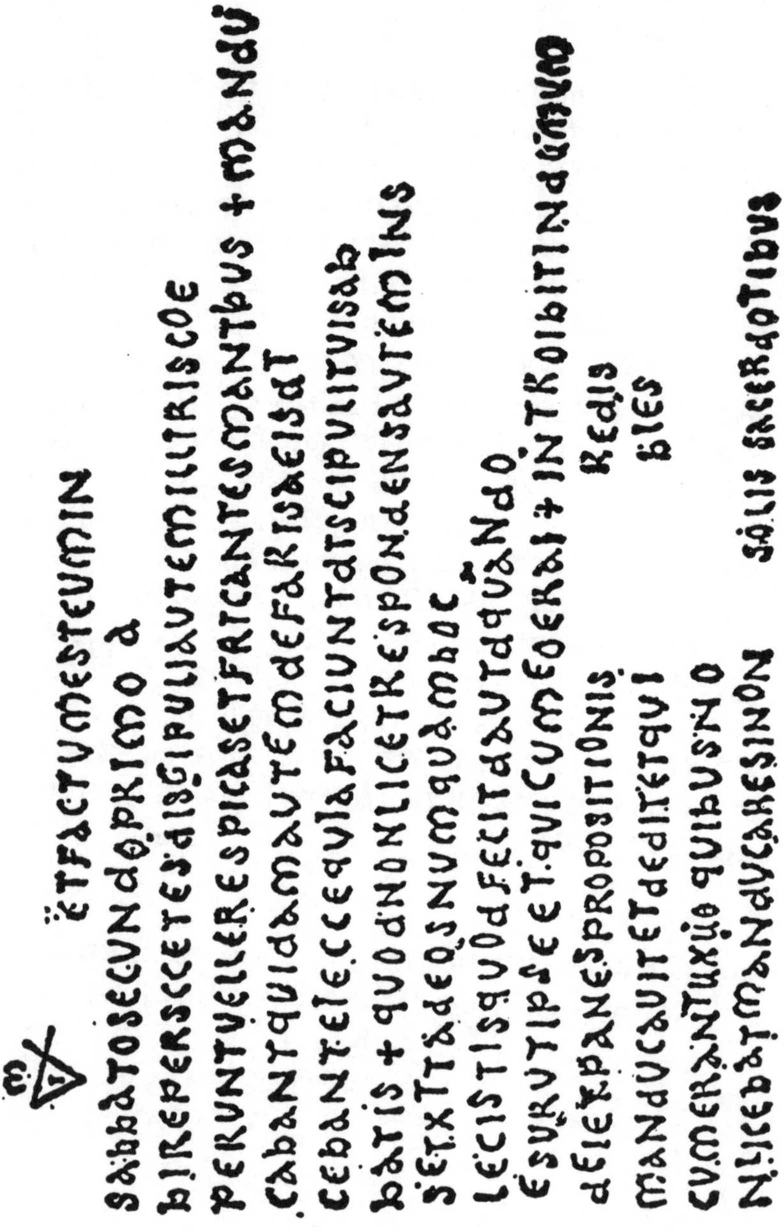

Fig.6. Manuscript II.

Thanks to the willingness of Commandant Lerville, President of the Association des Réservistes du Chiffre, I then sought assistance from several specialists in this branch of learning. I submitted the two manuscripts to them, together with accounts of the two tombstones and of the stone at Coumesourde, since I had a feeling that perhaps some relationship existed between the former and the latter.

At the conclusion of a highly technical study, they arrived at the following deductions:

1. The texts have been well encoded by means of a double key substitution, and then by a transposition effected by means of a chequer board.

2. In addition to the coding proper, the author has added rebuses.

3. Errors have been intentionally introduced so as to baffle any attempts at deciphering, the searcher being led along false trails.

It remained to pierce the disguise employed by the Machiavellian author of this brain-racking puzzle. According to Colonel Arnaud, Chief of the Army Signals Service and an eminent cryptographer, he was without doubt "…an ecclesiastic, brought up on Holy Scriptures, and loving mystery and fancy."

Since on one of the manuscripts is found the hieroglyph PS, which once appeared on the Marchioness of Blanchefort's tombstone, we can, without much risk of error, ascribe all these texts to the same author, namely: Abbé Antoine Bigou.

We would certainly have welcomed any documents relating to a person as singular as the Abbé Bigou. We have searched for information at his birthplace, Sournia (Pyrénées-Orientales). The reply from the Departmental Director of Archives for the region reads thus:

"All the documents relating to this region have been comprehensively withdrawn from the town-halls by a collector during the nineteenth century and all trace of them has been lost since that time."

But when all is said and done Antoine Bigou has only practised, albeit in a rather strange way, the art of cryptography. Someone was later to appear on the scene who would conceive and put into practice an enterprise that was truly fantastic. Having distorted a map that had appeared in a treatise on linguistics, he succeeded in falsifying the description of the whole of the landscape surrounding Rennes-les-Bains.

In appearance this man was nevertheless quite ordinary. Henri Boudet was born in 1837 at Quillan of a poverty-stricken family. His intelligence was exceptional, so he was very soon noticed by a wealthy ecclesiastic, Abbé de Cayron, who covered the cost of all his studies. The Abbé de Cayron was Curé of St Laurent de Cabrerisse in the Aude. Cayron's obituary published in the *Religious Weekly* of 1897 contains the following:

"He reconstructed his Church almost completely in beautiful gothic proportions and, apart from what the family of Rennes gave him, no one knew where he obtained money to cover the cost of such a major restoration."

Henri Boudet entered holy orders quite young, and in 1872 became Curé of Rennes-les-Bains. Poor but generous, he left with the faithful the memory of a saint, with the others that of a benefactor of the little town. He knew the district stone by stone and the learned journals of the Midi freely opened their columns to his works of erudition.

It was in 1886 that Henri Boudet published at Carcassonne *The True Celtic Language and the Cromlech of Rennes-les-Bains*. Reading this work a little too quickly, the first reaction will be an impulse to class the author in the category of "literary lunatic". In fact he declares without wincing that the mother tongue of humanity is that of the Celts. He asserts that this mother tongue has been maintained intact up to today in the twin tongues, English and Languedoc, from which by way of consequence, are derived all the other languages, Hebrew, Basque and Kabyle. The etymological examples cited to support this theory are certainly ingenious enough. Thus the Numides, so it appears, owe their name to the fact that the shepherds led their flocks to graze in fresh pastures, which in English would be "new meads".

Nevertheless some doubts must soon strike you; there is so much absurdity crowded onto each page, for no apparent reason. Is not all this meant to incite you to read the whole lot again, but this time between the lines? This new exercise, if one performs it carefully, will prove most instructive.

As the title itself makes clear, the etymological

fantasies are only a mask for the author; his real objective is geographical in nature. It is the description of the district, with its megalithic associations, of which Rennes-les-Bains forms the centre.

Engravings showing menhirs or rocks, in addition to a detailed map of the site, illustrate this apparent linguistic treatise. Moreover, as early as the first page, Boudet warns us, though not without humour,

"The study of the magnificent Celtic monument in existence at Rennes-les-Bains has led us with confidence to certain etymological deductions which to us seem difficult to refute." This will at once tell the reader that geography will be discussed, but in a coded language.

In principle, the coding system employed by Boudet is very simple. It was the author himself who exposed it to us in a transparent manner in the guise of a dissertation about a language that is pseudo-Punic; a pure product of his fancy:

"Note," he writes, "with what ease the Punic language can, by a play on words, manage to create the proper names of people. Common names also offer similar combinations and, by sequences of monosyllables, represent entire sentences with rigour and precision. We shall select some of these expressions so that one can see with what admirable ease the words, whether nouns or verbs, can be built up."

It cannot be said more plainly that the work is coded by means of a process that is dear, more particularly, to the hermeticists; that of the pun and play upon words. The pseudo-linguistic deviations have no purpose other than to mislead the inattentive reader and to alert the discerning reader.

They provide a way to conceal, within a work of three hundred and ten pages, a few key passages that are deciphered, whether purely phonetically like puns or by a play upon words, through deducing the figurative meaning which lies behind the apparent sense.

These passages are usually marked by the absurd introduction of a keyword.

As an example, take the word "Cayrolo" (a place-name often found in Languedoc). This comes from "caire" which denotes a squared stone, in Latin "quadrum". But Boudet pretends, against all the evidence, that "Cayrolo" comes from three English words, namely "key", "ear" and "hole". This enormity is only inserted in order to draw attention to the key passage, which follows immediately:

"Le Cayrolo des Redones, a silo or cavern containing the precious cereal, is situated to the south of Montferrand, quite close to the road leading to the Coume brook and to the Artigues. The production of wheat being really quite bounteous, they had recourse to foreign hands in these parts so that the harvest could be gathered in more speedily."

But as is well known, "wheat" is a slang term for "money". The cavern near Montferrand containing the precious cereal is therefore none other than an ancient mine located in that region and mentioned in the report of the prefect Barante. And in the foreign harvesters of long ago, the informed reader will easily recognise the German miners and metal workers summoned to this district by the Templars in the twelfth century.

In later pages, examples such as this become more frequent and soon the reader will ask,

"Whatever does Abbé Boudet wish to tell the happy few while he deceives a much larger number?"

The reply, stupefying as it may seem, is simply this. "The secret of a place, the precautions to take in order to reach it, and the silence to keep after its discovery."

As to the place, the work tells us almost everything. It is only accessible in certain seasons. One must go there alone and warmly clad. One must leave at sunrise and at first make one's way laboriously upwards. Then one continues the journey on much easier ground until a field is reached, then a spring, and then a fold full of sheep. There one must beware of being bitten by cattle ticks. Then there appears a natural cavern that one should not venture into thoughtlessly because entry is guarded by a dangerous cascade. It is risky to illuminate the cave. One's eyes will be filled with tears, but one must not rub them. One may perhaps break a leg.

Finally one will find there a horrifying spectacle, but one may indulge in plunder. One will come out with hair turned white. One must then respect the instructions, which order one to speak only with guarded words of what has happened. All this is set out on pages 120 to 126 of his strange work. Freed from its irrelevances, the text is in fact as follows:

January: bad weather stops the work. February: the warmth is enough to cause the ice to melt. March: continual rains turn the ground into a bog. July:

postpone all meetings or assemblies. August: the streams dry up. September: there is a wish to go to ground, to be shut up in caves. October: hurry through the work, cover oneself with woollen clothing.

Sunrise: man is tired out. Morning: walk with ease. Evening: run in haste to the dwelling.

A field. A spring: beginning to speed its flow. A pool: accelerate its flow. A hut: a crowd of heads under one roof; to kill with a pin those disgusting insects that start one itching. A house: to consider. A cellar: part of the house where one can drink oneself stupid. Thunder: see on high the lightning that is certain to do harm. Darkness: to quiet the insects' humming. The eye closes, as under the effect of a blow. Tears. To refuse what is necessary. To break ones leg. To utter cries of horror. To pillage. To be obliged to have white hair. To keep an eye on the instructions: to speak in a certain jargon to the outside world.

This laconic but intriguing itinerary, is only a sample of the many indications that teem within this volume. Only one thing is lacking, but as one might guess, it is the most important. Abbé Boudet has not told us where this dangerous and fascinating place that he describes, is to be found.

Certainly there is the map, the focal point of the book, which is only a commentary on it. But evidently we can hardly hope that the author will have written down in black and white the name of a place that he has taken so much care to conceal from the majority of his readers.

And in fact Abbé Boudet's cartography is no less subtle
than his linguistics. He has drawn a map, which is more
detailed than that of the 50,000 to 1 Ordnance Survey
map but which remains silent on certain matters. The
points not designated can however be fixed, since they
are located at the intersection of certain alignments. The
elements that permit these alignments to be determined
(like the numbers corresponding to longitudes, latitudes,
levels etc.) appear in the work. But they are scattered
and concealed[1].

Finally among these elements there appear dates,
since the author, using the cromlech as a gnomon, has
established the alignments as a function of the shadow
thrown by the sun onto certain reference marks. The
enormous complexity of the system can now be seen, as
well as the major difficulty of putting it into effect on the
ground. In fact, since the reference points have been
intentionally distorted in the map, we have to identify
on the terrain four accurately placed markers in order to
locate each reference point. The number of markers
needed to constitute a complete itinerary is therefore
very great.

But nature, which is chaotic and wild in the extreme
hereabouts, is no land surveyor. Providence has not laid
down around Rennes a series of convenient markers,
in sufficient numbers and in suitable positions. But Abbé

---

1. However, every time, there is placed an intentional anomaly by way of a
signal. Thus when the book is signed "H. Boudet", the map inserted therein
is signed "Edmund Boudet".

Boudet was not the sort of man to let his work be held up by so insignificant an obstacle. Does the countryside resist his plans? That cannot be allowed. It is not the plans that must be altered. The whole landscape must be modified.

Completing the strange path already sketched out by others before him, he traversed the mountainside tirelessly, setting up markers wherever he needed them. Not only did he mark out the Stations of the Cross, but also he took down and shifted the menhirs, re-modelled the silhouette of his church and even went so far as to modify several tombs in the cemetery at Rennes-les-Bains.

On this unusual trail, the curious traveller learns at each step some new rudiment of a strange language, where the words are sometimes a picture, sometimes a sculptured figure, sometimes a rock and sometimes even a projected shadow.

Dedicated to Saints Celse and Nazaire, the humble church of Rennes-les-Bains would seem at first sight to be unworthy of any attention. The place is however of venerable antiquity since a church was in existence under the same name patronage in the year 1162. If we go inside, a picture, which is unusual in the extreme, attracts us. It is a canvas donated at the beginning of the nine-teenth century by Marquis Paul-François-Vincent de Fleury de Blanchefort, who interested himself so much in the mines on his estates. The Son of Man is dead and lies still warm in a grotto, through the opening of which may be perceived a rock. On his left knee, the anonymous painter, by a skilful illusion, has depicted the head of a hare[1]. The left arm of Christ points to a tray upon which is placed a sphere. Below the tray there appears an enormous spider.

This picture has proved very intriguing to those who seek so passionately to solve the riddle of Rennes, even though sometimes they deny it. In the autumn of 1966, Mgr. Boyer, Vicar-General of the diocese of Carcassonne, M. Descadeillas, keeper of the city library, together with a constellation of learned men, went on a pilgrimage to this picture without succeeding in penetrating its secret.

Had they considered Henri Boudet's book and above all, had they shown a little childish fun in their approach, it would have allowed them to appreciate, without any false sense of shame, the play on words rather more easily. If such had been their frame of mind, and if they had known the topography of the district better, then the bizarre picture would have given up its message to them.

Rennes, which in bygone times was called Règnes, is flanked to the west and to the south-west by a plateau, whence flows the brook of the Dead Man. The riddle of the painter may therefore be simply read as follows:

"At Règnes (araigne) near the arm of the Dead Man who directs you towards the plateau, there lies the hare."

On entering the church one sees on the right a wrought iron cross decorated with rosettes, at the heart of which there appears, not Christ as might have been expected, but a Virgin and Child.

---

1. Translation note: The author uses "lièvre" here.

On the pedestal the following inscription may be read:

IN HOC SIGNO VINCES

———————

DOMINO VIE RECTORE

———————

PETRUS DELMAS FECIT

1856

Knowing that in this region it is the cross that has been employed as a reference point, let us examine this one more closely. Decorated with roses, it first displays the coat of arms of the person who set it up and had the inscription engraved. Without offending against what is seemly in this place, perhaps we can then permit ourselves to hum the words of a song, which made Gilbert Bécaud popular:

I have written these few lines

So as to indicate to you:

The important thing is the rose, believe me.

From the somewhat cryptic French:

J'ai écrit ces quelques lignes

Comme pour te faire signe:

L'important, c'est la rose crois-moi.

What draws the eye in the inscription is the phrase: DOMINO VIE RECTORE. Word for word, this can be translated to read "To Seigneur Vié, Rector", or perhaps "Erected during the rectorship of Seigneur Vié." And in fact the Curé of Rennes-les-Bains was named Jean Vié. However it is hardly common practice for a Calvary to be dedicated to the Curé, above all while he is still alive. Nor is it customary in Languedoc for the Curé to be called Rector as in Brittany. Still more improbable is it for him to be given the title of Seigneur. The existence of so many obvious anomalies must present us with a double meaning. But the second meaning will only appear if you read the phrase out loud, for DOMINO VIÆ RECTORE means "To the master who shows the way."

In order to reveal this "via", which, by poor play on words, should lead us to Master Vié, it is enough for us to follow the very simple advice IN HOC SIGNO VINCES. These words would prompt us while standing before the Calvary, to make the Sign of the Cross, as all the faithful would instinctively do. That is to say, we would trace out a pattern in the form of a figure "4". Here, when facing the Calvary, we have the west in front of us and the east behind us. Making the Sign of the Cross will therefore consist of the following actions.

1. Tracing a line east–west,

2. Turning to the left forty-five degrees to our path, towards the south-east.

3. Turning again through forty-five degrees, which will place us facing north-east[1].

Having done this, we shall observe that on the ground each of the three branches of the Sign of the Cross (or

---

1. Translation note: Practical application differs.

if you prefer it the figure "4") is directed towards monuments that are as singular as they are distinctive.

The first branch (east–west) points successively to a lime tree and a tomb situated in the cemetery, the Calvary "DOMINO VIE RECTORE", and far off hidden from our view by the contour of the land, a stone cross placed in the open country.

The second branch (north-west–south-east) leads us from the Calvary to another tomb. Finally the third branch (south–north) leads us from this last tomb to the picture of Christ with the hare, and thence to a stone head embedded in the wall of the presbytery. When on the actual site we cannot follow the route in the order of the shape of a "4", because the walls will stop us at several points.

Since we cannot pass through the walls, let us take map and compass in hand.

Leaving the lime tree and facing west, before us there is a strange tomb.

On it may be read,

Here lies

Jean VIE

born in 1808

Appointed Curé in 1840

Died on the 1st September 1872

Pray for him.

There he is again then, our friend Vié, who is supposed to indicate to us the way to go! What first catches ones eye is the exceedingly unusual format used here to write 1st September, namely "le 1er 7bre", which places in prominence the number 17. Can we still invoke chance for this? No, because Jean Vié did not die on 1st September. (We have taken the trouble to verify this in the *State Civil Registers*).

There remains only one solution, that with which someone decidedly wants us to become familiar, namely that of the rebus and the pun. The writer has skilfully suggested a date, which is the same as that which we have already noticed on the enigmatic tomb of the Marchioness de Blanchefort and which we shall soon find again though sometimes in different forms — 17 January.

RENNES-LES-BAINS. List of places.

1. Lime tree.
2. Vié tomb.
3. Calvary, showing the way.
4. Stone cross.
5. Second Fleury tomb.
6. Picture.
7. Head of Dagobert (or of the Saviour)
8. Boudet tomb and first Fleury tomb.
9. Grating.
10. Sphere.
11. Decapitated menhir (Cap de l'Hom).
12. Church of Rennes-le-Château.

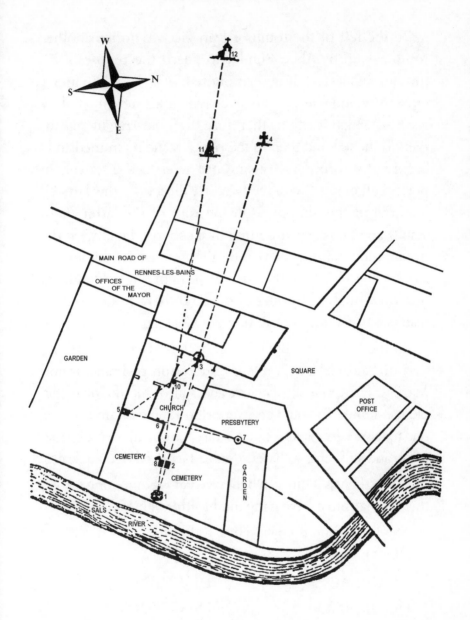

Fig.7. Rennes-les-Bains.

To the left of the tomb of Jean Vié, we notice another tomb set up by Abbé Boudet to guard the repose of his mother and sister. It is surmounted by a cross, the upper extremity and the two arms of which are terminated by arrows, which invite us therefore, to look straight ahead, then to the left and then to the right. Standing immediately before the tomb and raising our eyes, we discover, in perfect alignment with the westerly direction, the latticed window of the church. On the roof of the latter there stands an obelisk surmounted by a sphere. Finally, on the distant mountainside there is the decapitated menhir known as Cap de l'Hom. In the same alignment but hidden from our view by the contours of the land there lies, in the far distance, the church of Rennes-le-Château.

To the left of the Boudet tomb, there is another tomb, that of Paul-Urbain de Fleury, grandson of François and Marie d'Hautpoul-Blanchefort and son of the donor of the picture-rebus. It would be a very remarkable occurrence for one to have a double life, but it is rare for one to have a double tomb and still rarer to have a double birth and double death.

Nevertheless if one can believe what is before one's eyes, this is what must have happened to this gentleman.

The first stone is engraved as follows:

CI GIT PA	CI GIT PA
UL URBAIN	UL URBAIN
DE FLEURY	DE FLEURY
NE LE 3 MAI	DECEDE LE
1776	7 AOUT
	1836

A little further away to the right, on the other hand, a second stone declares:

IL EST PASSE EN FAISANT LE BIEN

Restes transférés

de Paul-Urbain Comte de FLEURY

décédé le 7 août 1856

à l'âge de 60 ans

If Paul-Urbain died in 1856 at the age of sixty as the second stone affirms, he cannot have been born in 1776, as the first stone states, but in 1796. If he was born in 1776 as the first[1] stone affirms, he cannot have been sixty years old at his death in accordance with the second stone but eighty.

In reality Paul-Urbain de Fleury was born neither in 1776 nor in 1796 but in 1778.

Double tombstones, double inscriptions on the first stone and double dates.

By this insistence, are we intended to understand that Paul-Urbain, beyond his ordinary birth and death, experienced the death followed by the symbolic rebirth that represents the initiation, thus "passed by doing good works", as is required of Adepts? Does someone want to point out to us that a deposit belonging to Fleury has been "transferred" and that we must interpret these false dates as being numerical indications?

This would be sufficiently in the style of those who have painted, sculptured, or chronicled every aspect of Rennes.

---

1. Translation note: The original text states "la seconde" here.

On the other hand, should good sense protect us from such risky interpretation and compel us to ignore these errors as being only simple oversights? This last solution would surely be the most reasonable... if we had not previously examined the tomb on the right.

"Abbé Boudet's book is a pure fantasy which should be held in low esteem," so the condescending and even the erudite have told me. However, one cannot believe this to be the advice expressed by everybody. Today in fact this book cannot be found except by a lucky chance. The copy that exists in the Carcassonne library is badly worn, so much has it been read, and it cannot be borrowed under any pretext. At the National Library it appears in the catalogue, certainly, but you cannot read it, because it has been stolen.

Some very restricted societies holding copies still exist, but they keep these strictly guarded and preserved in their locked cupboards.

ooOOoo

Since the alignment so wisely provided by Abbé Boudet invites us there, let us leave for Rennes-le-Château. Only one road lies before us, that via Couiza. While in this little town, let us cast a glance at the monument to the dead, placed within the church, which location is in itself unusual. To our great surprise we see there the same rebus as appears on the bizarre picture of the descent from the Cross. Here again the arm of the dead man points to a stone, which is round like a loaf of bread. Without a doubt, someone is being insistent and even specific.

This very curious monument deserves our detailed examination. The soldier, hand on knee with left knee uncovered, is shown in the traditional pose of initiation. Veiled by the national flag, there is seen a dried-up tree, only one branch of which is still living. It is crowned with an angel tied to an anchor, an emblem of faith.

At Rennes-le-Château, the group of buildings designed by Bérenger Saunière and above all the multitude of unusual and disturbing personages that he has conjured up within his church, grows oppressive, so very like the atmosphere of the little village. Here everything seems to have been arranged with an insane attention to detail so as to suggest a mystery while at the same time provoking revulsion towards it.

Is this an accursed place? Cursed by whom? When? Why? Must we accept to the letter the warning that is given to us in Latin on the porch of St Mary Magdalene, "Terribilis est locus iste"? Such questions are vain and even childish, but in spite of everything, they still gush forth. But in fact, we can ignore the questionable taste of this assemblage, because that aspect is, in reality, negligible compared to the lofty objectives for which Bérenger spent a fortune in remodelling and decorating his church.

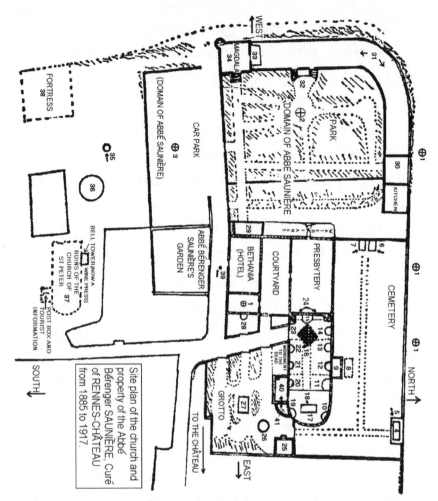

Fig.8. Rennes-le-Château - Church and Domain.

RENNES-LE-CHÂTEAU. List of places:

1. Excavations made in 1964.
2. Excavations to 18 metres.
3. Excavations to 17 metres.
4. Stone defaced by Bérenger Saunière.
5. Ossuary.
6. Tomb of Abbé Bérenger Saunière.
7. Tomb of Marie Denarnaud.

RENNES-LE-CHÂTEAU. List of places (continued):
  8. Tomb of Hautpoul-Blanchefort Ladie(s).
  9. Bell tower.
  10. Saint Joseph.
  11. Throne.
  12. Saint Anthony the Hermit.
  13. Saint Germaine.
  14. Saint John the Baptist.
  15. Confessional.
  16. Chessboard.
  17. Altar.
  18. Mary Magdalene tableau.
  19. The Virgin Mary.
  20. Saint Anthony of Padua.
  21. Saint Mary Magdalene.
  22. Saint Roch.
  23. The devil Asmodeus.
  24. Large tableau.
  25. Repository for the dead.
  26. Ancient baptismal urn.
  27. Calvary.
  28. Our Lady of Lourdes.
  29. Chapel of Abbé Bérenger Saunière.
  30. Orangery.
  31. Terrace or belvedere.
  32. Staircase and pond.
  33. Veranda.
  34. Magdala tower.
  35. Ancient pits (blocked up).
  36. Water tower.
  37. Ruins of Saint Peter's Church.
  38. Site of fortress.
  39. Ancient pits (blocked up).
  40. Sacristy.
  41. Small secret room.

Being a faithful disciple of Abbé Boudet, what Saunière has left us, under the guise of pious iconography, is a trail of misleading fabrication, craftily alluding to the places he has explored and the secrets that he has extracted from them.

For this purpose, he has employed a language of metaphors and allegories, which remains impenetrable to the stranger, but which can be read fluently by whoever is well acquainted with both the history of Rennes and with the place names of the district.

So his church seems to remind us of the famous story by Edgar Allen Poe, in which a letter could not be found because it was too obviously displayed. But Saunière, perhaps inspired by others, did not stop there. His clear intention was, and he has succeeded so well in this, that reading his cartographic message should generate, as if in counterpoint, a whole bundle of symbols. Such symbols would allow the initiated visitor to discern the statement of esoteric belief that characterises the whole collection and identifies its authors. We shall mention the latter aspect only in passing. It is mainly the invitation to retrace Bérenger's strange journey that holds our interest.

Every geographic map is the representation of a whole landscape by means of conventional symbols. In order to read it and thus to orientate oneself on the terrain, one must know the significance of these symbols. They become much more numerous and complex as the map gets more detailed. An ordnance survey map remains silent to the uninitiated. To learn to read it is a very lengthy process. Student officers spend months of hard work before attaining proficiency.

On an ordnance survey map for example, concentric hatching represents a rounded hillock. If an uninitiated person is asked,

"What do you see there?", he will reply,

"Hatching." If, to show the hill, one had simply drawn the nipple of either a man or woman, then even a child of ten would have answered,

"A breast."

Now it is this last procedure, analogous to the technique of the map designer but basically much simpler, that has been employed by Bérenger Saunière. The cleverness lies in the possibility that this will pass undetected because nobody or hardly anybody will imagine that any religious statue could possibly conceal cartography. However, here this is indeed the case. A searching visit will progressively cause us to become convinced of this underlying symbolism.

Standing before the church, perched upon the superb Visigothic pillar, the eye is immediately caught by a Virgin of Lourdes in stucco, distressing in its ugly banality. Such statues were moulded in their thousands at about that time.

We have the inclination to pass by without further thought, but let us give it our attention. Rather, let us read the inscription carved upon the pedestal:

"PENITENCE, PENITENCE." These words, which have not been chosen by chance, inform us that this particular Virgin is not that of Lourdes as would first seem apparent. This is because the Virgin of Lourdes said to Bernadette Soubirous,

"I am the immaculate conception," whereas, "Pénitence, Pénitence" are the exact words spoken by another Virgin, who in 1846 appeared in tears to two young shepherds at La Salette near Grenoble. From the little that we know of it, this false quotation will put us on the alert.

If we are well read, we may recall the opening pages of *La Cathédrale,* in which Huysmans traced out the opposition between the Virgin of Lourdes and the Virgin of La Salette. The former is the "Virgin for everybody, a Virgin for the village altar, a Madonna of the Saint-Sulpice quarter, a queen of the street corner"; the latter is the "Virgin for more important people, for mystics and for artists." "The Virgin of Lourdes enters laughing, and never prophesies catastrophe." On the other hand, the Virgin of La Salette will deliver an apocalyptic message. Here then, we are offered two Marys in one, the first concealing the other. We shall then remember that there is, in the neighbour- hood, a small river called the Sals. Salette, Sals; there is surely a subtle allusion but one that is unequivocal.

But, through her tears, Mary of la Salette calls to mind a third Mary — Mary Magdalene. Now where the Sals receives the waters of the Blanque may be found a spring called The Well of Magdalene. Here is another allusion to confirm and consolidate the first.

The Virgin of La Salette announced to the young shepherds a widespread war, Marseilles ruined by earth- quakes, Paris burning, the partial depopulation of the world.

It is true that this terrifying story was blessed with a successful conclusion: the restoration of the French monarchy appeasing forever the wrath of God. At the time when Saunière was exercising his talents this prophecy aroused a wave of agitation in various politico-mystical circles.

The Legitimists, and even more so the smaller sects, Naundorffists and others, haunted by the old theme of the "lost king", found in this a confirmation of their hopes[1]. Here is mingled the eternal millennium dream, for, with Péladan, Catholic occultism was in fashion, and Barrès himself dabbled in it. Under her soothing exterior, the Virgin of Rennes-le-Château does not only show us the road to follow; she also shows us an atmosphere where intrigue and plot are blended with religious speculation. The Master of Works has thus killed two birds with one stone.

This atmosphere is manifest again, even more clearly, on the tympanum of the church. There, roses alternate with crosses; a rebus accessible to anyone who comes along: "Rose-Cross". Below and to the right a heraldic lily (fleur-de-lys) within a circle, decorates a stone that has been taken

---

1. According to the evangelists, Jesus was, through his maternal lineage, a descendant of David and Solomon, and so King of the Jews through his royal blood. That supposition has fuelled speculations as to the possible survival of the privileged human line of descent into which the Messiah was incarnated, these speculations being reinforced by the incontestable analogy between the anointing of the Jewish kings and the sacred unction introduced by Clovis. The dogma of the Immaculate Conception, resulting from the miracle of Lourdes, radically undermined these ideas by elevating Mary above the natural order. So it is not surprising that the politico-mystical sects should prefer La Salette to Lourdes.

from the original structure. This motif, duly repeated in
the interior, proves that, well before Saunière, builders or
benefactors of this sanctuary made explicit allusion to the
cromlech of Rennes-les-Bains, for a cromlech is a stone
circle surrounding a central stone. In the toponomy of the
region the word "lys," (in Latin, lesia) indicates a raised
stone. But it is also made clear that they were not ignorant
of the sestet of Nostradamus entitled, *The Ring and the Lily.*

As soon as you have passed through the church door, a
group, surprising at the very least, welcomes us. A hideous
devil carved, painted, and life-size, supports the basin for
holy water. He seems to be sitting though a seat cannot be
seen. His right leg is deformed, and he has laid the five
fingers of his left hand upon his knee. The thumb and the
index finger of his right hand join forming a circle. The
knotted muscles of his chest are hardly in accordance
with anatomy; one side being flattened while the nipple
is displaced.

The stoup that he supports is surmounted by a scroll
bearing the initials B.S. and flanked by two heraldic figures
— basilisks. Above the whole structure there are four
angels, each of whom makes one of the Signs of the Cross,
accompanied by the inscription,

"Par ce signe tu le vaincras"; "By this sign shalt thou
conquer him."

We know very well that this strange group, this artificial
assemblage of elements having hardly any connection with
each other, is in reality some kind of hieroglyph.

The lameness of the devil shows us at one and the same time his name and what he has come here to do; as everyone knows, the lame devil is Asmodeus. Now the Bible and the Jewish commentary known under the name of *Midrashim,* teach us that it was to him that Solomon entrusted the guardianship of the cave that contained his treasure. One day, the King being deprived of his seal, the demon forbade him access to the grotto. It was only when Solomon had found his jewelled ring again, that he was able to chase Asmodeus into the desert. Bérenger, by making his devil lame, tells us clearly which subject he wishes us to keep in mind. But we have not forgotten about the treasure, which the local legend said was guarded by the devil close to Blanchefort, and was the subject about which the Marquis de Fleury would have started a law case, since his estates had been trespassed upon.

If we are now overcome by curiosity, an area to be prospected can be indicated to us with some certainty. In fact, for little more than naming them out loud, each detail of the monument indicates a place in the neighbourhood. Let us therefore name them.

The devil seems to be sitting down: a rock exists named the devil's armchair.

Two of his fingers form a circle: a spring exists named Spring of the Circle.

One of his sides is flat: there exists near benchmark 530 of the ordnance survey map, a place called Le Pla de la Coste.

The nipple has been misplaced: there is a place called Devil's Breast mentioned by Catel, on the site of an old signal tower; "sein" here being a corruption of "signe", in Latin "signum".

The devil supports the stoup, which is topped by the initials B.S. There is a place called Le Bénitier (stoup), just between the Blanque and Sals rivers. Bérenger Saunière has here cleverly played upon his own initials.

Finally, the devil places his five fingers upon his knee: on the rock called the Breadstone are hollowed out five little cups like the imprint of five fingers. This is called the devil's hand. But here Saunière has been subtle. The rebus is in stages, and indicates a date. Cinq (five) and genou (knee) gives in fact Saint Genou, whose Saint day is the 17th January!

A glance at the map allows us to state that all the places thus indicated are approximately orientated on the monument, relative to each other, just as they are on the ground. Therefore, the most incredulous should agree with us that any accumulation of chance circumstances must be ruled out.

The motto carved below the angels: "By this sign shalt thou conquer him" should now receive our attention once more. Let us, as at Rennes-les-Bains, make use of the advice given to us to follow. From the monument before which we now stand the route indicated in step four of the Sign of the Cross will lead us first towards the porch, then, crossing a paved area, towards the baptismal fonts. However, we are well aware that, wherever and whenever we see it, the translation of the famous "In hoc signo vinces" is "By this sign shalt thou conquer". By adding "him" or "it" Saunière has reinforced his indication. What is necessary to be conquered is certainly the devil, the obstacle protecting the treasure.

This addition now also results in a phrase of twenty-two letters, the same number as in the phrase: "Reddis regis cellis arcis" on the Blanchefort tomb and in the phrase: "Terribilis est locus iste" on the porch, which makes allusion to a cave which is equally mysterious and formidable.

Inasmuch as it can hardly be considered an expert translation, the inscription,

CELLIS ARCIS

REDDIS REGIS

signifies, if read horizontally,

"At royal Rennes, in the caves of the fortress" or if read vertically,

"Make restitution by the caves, govern by the coffers."

At the same time as he carved the warning on the porch, "This place is terrible," Saunière carved "God will hear my prayer" and "My house will be called a house of prayer," an evangelical quotation, which is followed by "now you have made it a den of thieves". Taking account of the language that remains unspoken, one may suspect an allusion to a subterranean place, whether temple or cave, formidable in its access and containing (just like the robbers' cave in Ali Baba, which needed a "Sesame" to gain access) a precious treasure.

The number 22, to which our attention has been drawn, is by no means commonplace. It is the number of letters in the Hebrew alphabet, and for that reason always lends itself to numerological, mythical or occult speculation. Number 22, amongst other things (and the builders of this unusual place cannot have ignored it), is one of the mystery cards of the Tarot pack, the one named Mat (check-mate). Can this then be really a game of chess that must be won, your opponent being the devil?

If we follow the direction in which the devil is looking, we notice in fact that he is staring at the black and white tiled paving, which has been placed so as to emphasise a chess board of sixty-four squares, the corners of which are orientated towards the cardinal points. In Saunière's time, only this part of the paving was in existence; the remaining tiles have since been added.

Positioned opposite the devil and near the baptismal fonts, a stucco figure of Jesus being baptised by John also stares at the chessboard. The two characters, goat and scapegoat, the devil green on a red pedestal, the Christ red on a green pedestal, certainly in opposition but also complementary, meditate over an invisible game, which cannot be played unless both are present, but to which each of them proposes his own solution.

Before the baptismal fonts, ritual will require the faithful once more to make the Sign of the Cross. This serves to lead us first to the confessional, which is surmounted by an immense picture, then towards the altar.

Already well initiated in Saunière's allegoric language,

we shall have no difficulty in reading on the confessional
another allusion to the tradition of the gold of Rennes.
Adjoining the chessboard, this confessional is decorated
by a woodcarving, depicting the Good Shepherd bringing
back the lost sheep. Certainly, this evangelical reference is
appropriate here.

But it reminds us also of the young shepherd Paris, who
in 1646 found, so it seems, the treasure while seeking one
of his sheep, which had strayed down into a grotto. This is
still what we think of when we read on the façade of the
presbytery,

"The house of the shepherd is the house for all." In fact
this maxim indicates in disguised words a precise location;
the ruins of the house of the shepherd Paris which can still
be seen to the south-east of Rennes-les-Bains, perched on
a height like an observatory. Just above the confessional,
as if to stress the directions still more, a picture painted
and carved in semi-relief occupies the whole of the upper
part of the wall.

There we see Jesus consoling the suffering, a theme that
is not at all unusual in a church. However, here again it is
the details that we shall find to be the most revealing.

Jesus is seen to be at the summit of a flower-clad hillside,
which slopes sharply and is covered with bushes. On the
ground, well in sight, there is a very large bag, shaped like
a purse and punctured with a great hole. Now the artist
has not failed to locate this flowery landscape. Two scenes
serve as a border. The one to the left can be recognised,
since in the foreground there is the Bread Stone and on

the horizon the rocks of Pla de la Coste, called the Rollers, and the ruins of Blanchefort. That on the right depicts the rock shaped like the "gaming die" of the Serbaïrou district, and some ruins in the background that seem to be those of Coustaussa. Finally the confessional cross has been placed so that we can see it at the bottom of the landscape.

How better could we be invited to search over the whole neighbourhood of Rennes-les-Bains (the thermal baths where the sick are comforted) for a flowery terrain (that is to say, land which once belonged to the Fleury family) steep, covered by bushes, marked by a cross and giving cover to the entrance to a cave, which like a purse, contains a precious deposit?

A third allusion to this underground place is now offered to us beneath the altar, which was the theatre for Saunière's first discovery, the manuscripts. There, below the table, we see a picture in a naïve style, to which Saunière attached so much importance that he painted it himself. Mary Magdalene is kneeling in a grotto, the opening of which allows one to see the rock of Blanchefort opposite the peak of Cardou, and a rock that brings to mind a human profile having a prominent nose. At her hips she wears a little red apron in the shape of a heart, which she encompasses with hands joined, the fingers being interlaced, so as to form a grille, requiring an unusual contortion. At her feet there is a human skull; by her side an open book marked with two crosses and some illegible inscriptions. Before her there is a crude cross formed by two dry branches, while from the upright of this cross there emerges another small branch, which is also dried up.

The Saint's eyes are staring at the centre of the cross. Beneath this picture there is an inscription, the text of which has been borrowed from one of the manuscripts found by Saunière. It will be noted that the writing is peculiar:

JÉSU.MEDÈLA.VULNÉRUM + SPES.UNA.PŒNITENTIUM.
PER.MAGDALENÆ.LACRYMAS ÷ PECCATA.NOSTRA.DILUAS.

In Latin, this inscription would not normally bear either accents, or dots above the letter I. Now it includes four such letters, which cause the syllables JE, DE, NE and NI to become evident. Again it is a matter of a rebus, whereby one should read JAIS, DÉ, NEZ and NID, which conceal certain topographical directions.

JAIS: a jet mine, the entrance to which Boudet found beneath a dolmen marked by a cross, exists near Sougraignes.

DÉ: a raised stone shaped like a gaming die exists near Serbaïrou.

NEZ: a rock shaped like the nose in the picture, also exists on the terrain, near Peyrolles.

NID: the highest point of the region is the Eagle's Nest of Cardou, which is rich in kaolin.

Let us note that, like the Christ with the hare of Rennes-les-Bains, the character in the picture has been shown in a grotto, the entrance of which discloses an exact landscape.

Before persons unknown had mutilated it, the grotto of rocks constructed by Saunière in his church garden undoubtedly formed a faithful model of this grotto whose existence is so persistently pointed out to us. Here the position of the picture beneath the altar would seem to suggest that the entrance to the grotto might well be located below the stone slab of a dolmen[1].

The allusion to the place called Magdalene's Spring, (Magdalenæ Lacrymas) is significant. Now consider this together with the reference to the place called the Dead Man (denoted by the skull), the grille and the earnest gaze towards a narrow passage, implying the strait and narrow path to follow. This could be, on the terrain, "the only hope of the penitent" seeking to slip into the cave, so completing the clues to the overall scheme.

Before the altar, a third Sign of the Cross is required of the faithful. This time it leads to the statue of Saint Anthony the Hermit. This will indicate to us another place in the district, the Hermit's Grotto, the entrance to which is by the Dead Man. In addition, the investigator who makes his visit here at the right time of the year will perceive, not without surprise, that the sun's rays shining through the open window onto the wall opposite, will fall exactly on the statue when it is 17th January. This is the saint's day for Anthony the Hermit. Here once again is something that must exclude coincidence.

---

1. This guidance is repeated in a peculiar stained glass window in the church, which represents the meal at Emmaus, in which Magdalene can be seen hiding under the table.

The final movement in the Sign of the Cross will lead us to the sacristy. There, two moral injunctions, one on either side of a mirror, declare,

BEFORE MASS and AFTER MASS respectively, to remind us that the Priest must wash his hands before and after administering the sacrament. But above all we shall discover that the wall cupboard intended for the storage of the sacramental ornaments is a deception, since it possesses a false panel. This conceals a door leading to a secret room, a small quadrant-shaped enclosure feebly lit by a circular, bull's-eye window.

We shall remember that it was in this sacristy that Bérenger double-locked himself each evening, after his long wandering over the mountain with a basket on his back. One can well imagine that he would celebrate for himself a sort of secret liturgy of gold. The window, covered by a black curtain would shield him from the unwanted gaze of indiscreet onlookers. No doubt it was with respect and suitably cleansed, as if he were about to approach the altar, that he handled the noble metal. He was one upon whom Christian ritual had bestowed the privilege of touching consecrated bread and wine, the body and the blood of Christ, and the metal which the first Magus offered to the infant Jesus.

"Receive, O King, gold, the symbol of royalty."

Then, his task completed, the gold hidden away, and the curtain raised, Bérenger had to remove all traces of his labour, both around him and on his hands, which he again washed as after the Mass.

But later, as he set out for home, passing through his church now plunged in shadows, the ironic gaze of Asmodeus seated near the porch would have reminded him that gold is also a vile and squalid metal. Gold, which inspires baseness and crime, and which, though pure when in the hands of the Magus, can yet be the wages of betrayal when taken into the hands of Judas.

After celebrating this golden Mass, the Curé — prisoner to his secret — doubtless only found sleep troubled by the conflict between ambition, remorse and fear.

Every church contains what is the equivalent of a labyrinth, which is the Way of the Cross. This sequence of pictures is in fact a pilgrimage for those who are unable to make their way to the Holy Land. It is also a symbolic journey that the faithful are invited to traverse on each Good Friday — at the hour when Christ trod the rocky road to Golgotha. At each station of the Cross all must chant the Stabat Mater. "Fix the wounds of the crucified one firmly within my heart."

By its very nature, the Way of the Cross is admirably suited to what is depicted there, in allegorical form, as guide-markers relating to a very definite journey. Let us see whether such is the case in the church at Rennes-le-Château.

The term "Way of the Cross" tells us at once that on the map as well as on the ground the way is marked by means of the crosses that Abbé Boudet laid out in the area surrounding Rennes as the stages and signposts of an enigmatic guidebook. Red crosses have been carved on the rocks at Cugulhou, at Roulers and at Cap de l'Hom, while Calvaries serve as reference points at Coustaussa, at the bridge over the Sals and at Jaffus etc. Now, looking carefully at the sequence of pictures that we have before us, we shall discover that, faithful to his own method of imaginative map-making, it is surely along this Way of the Cross that Bérenger Saunière is leading us.

He warns us at the same time that this road resembles the Way of the Cross though it is partly below the earth. The searcher who undertakes the task will suffer to the limit of his endurance, as did Jesus at Calvary; above all he will, in the same way, bear a heavy burden. Perhaps he will suffer even more, since Veronica will not be there to wipe his forehead, nor Cyrenius to comfort him.

Also, to make the indications even clearer, statues of saints are carefully chosen by reason of the associated legends. These are placed between the pictures as if to underline their significance.

For fear of trying the patience of the reader, we shall not analyse all fourteen Stations of the Cross one by one. Our purpose is not to draw up an exhaustive inventory but rather to show by examples what methods those responsible for this bizarre activity employed to deliver their message.

We shall limit ourselves to certain examples that illustrate the procedure employed and demonstrate the overall meaning. Then once inside Bérenger Saunière's church you can, if you so wish, use your own wits on the remaining pictures, which for lack of time we have passed over.

Saint Anthony the Hermit, whom we have picked out already, is taken as an example. Suggesting grottoes, he reminds us that this part of the journey is taken below ground. Placed between the first station and the last, he shows us that the journey is circular, so that one comes out where one has entered.

The first station of the Way of the Cross, the judgement of Pilate, is located, like the other monuments we have examined, on the geographic plan by which our journey should be traced. Immediately the eye is attracted by an unusual detail. The procurator of Judea does not wash his hands in a basin, but in a white tray held by a Negro suggesting Blanchefort and Roco Negro. Here again we shall find a topographic rebus very similar to that which appears on the strange "Christ with the hare" of Rennes-les-Bains. So here is provided another example of the goals and procedures that are prescribed for us.

Indications of a similar nature are to be read at the sixth station. There, a soldier raises his shield revealing a half-hidden tower and a dome. Veronica offers the linen cloth to mop Jesus' brow while Simon-Peter is looking on. The whole picture shows us exactly how it is to be orientated on the ground in the form of a complete rebus which we leave you to solve when you feel so inclined.

If we look carefully at the set of fourteen stations, we shall notice that in each picture, the earth is shown as being of a different colour; now it is white, then black, then mottled; sometimes it is flattened, sometimes irregular. Nothing would seem to justify the reason for these variations introduced by the painter, except the need to present to us, as if in a scale model, the sequence of features that the terrain offers to the explorer on his journey. In the same way, the various bodily positions assumed by Christ, representing the traveller himself, together with those of the subsidiary characters, indicate the various postures that the varying terrain forces the searcher to adopt. Here one can hold oneself erect, but elsewhere one must stoop, fall on ones knees, or crawl in the mud. Here one can stay clothed while elsewhere it will be necessary to undress, etc.

At the third station for example Jesus, on his knees, is shifting a heavy stone with his two hands. This action is not mentioned in any of the evangelical accounts. It has only been included here to indicate to us a narrow passage that can be negotiated only on ones knees and where the way is blocked by a large stone, which must be moved.

At the fourth station, the traveller can stand erect but, as is shown by the gesture of the soldier, he finds himself faced by a dead-end path. It is towards a curtain of dripping water behind him, symbolised by Magdalene in tears, that he directs his gaze, suggesting to us that this is the path to follow. Having arrived at this point one loses sight of the entrance.

Between the third and fourth stations the statue of St Germaine of Pibrac has been placed. This shepherdess of Languedoc is supposed to have lived at the end of the sixteenth century, but her existence is so suspect that it was not until 1867 that she achieved canonisation. It is

related that she gave alms, unbeknown to her cruel step-
mother, who was therefore scandalised when she took bread
to the poor, and so forced her to open her apron; but the
bread had already been turned into roses. It is also told
how she used to go far into the country to pray on her
knees in the mud before a bush, and that one day the arm
of a stream dried up miraculously giving her a dry passage
across. Long after St Germaine's death, her body was found
intact but afflicted by a deformity; one of her arms being
shrivelled up and desiccated.

To the historian of religions, this legend is only a be-
lated copy of that of St Roseline of Villeneuve. Here for
the visitor interested in allegories, Germaine, who tended
sheep, just like Ignace Paris, is not only included with
her roses and bush in the picture of the flowery (Fleury)
landscape, but the imagery is also strengthened by the
indication of Christ on his knees in the mud. Finally, she
seems to point out to the traveller that he should look out
for the dried up arm of a watercourse.

At the tenth station, several details strike us. The
wanderer is stripped of his clothes. As we are shown in the
picture this is because he has to hurry down a wall of rock
beneath a waterfall to reach a lower chamber. The soldier
on the right, by his posture indicates the place where,
having come so far, he has next to place his foot. The
soldier on the left, whose head projects from the picture
frame, the better to attract our attention, draws lots for
the seamless garment. See his hand holding the dicing
cup. It reproduces exactly the gesture made by Asmodeus

at the stoup. Notice also the gaming dice, enormously enlarged so that we can read the spots, five and seven, which seem to indicate a measure, perhaps that of the paces that are to be taken.

This station is separated from the succeeding one by a statue of St Roch. This saint (who seems never to have existed) was born, so it is said, having a red cross mark upon his chest. Being a pilgrim he lived through an epidemic plague by tracing the Sign of the Cross. The malady did not spare him, and he saved his life by enduring a suppurating sore on his upper thigh. By his name and the legend, this fictitious character is very peculiar and also very rich in symbolic echoes. His name, Roch, comes from rubeus, meaning red, and refers to the colour of the cross with which he was marked at birth. It is a curious fact that this was also that by which the Merovingian kings could be recognised at birth as being of the royal line. Here in a very definite manner, the saint announces at the same time a rock marked by a red cross and also a dripping opening.

These few examples, let me repeat, do not exhaust the examination of this church, unique of its kind. We only provide them so that the reader may accustom himself to a language that is cryptic and dream-like, but, like this one, is also coherent and precise. When familiar with this district and with its history and with his eyes wide open to the clues, the traveller (such as perhaps you will be) may read the signs on a once silent map. Thus he may become to some degree the psychoanalyst of Bérenger Saunière and of those mysterious ones who so inspired him.

Who could these have been? Probably a Rosicrucian sect. The roses and crosses carved on the porch are not the only indications of this. In a curious work, a Rosicrucian author, Jacques Duchaussoy[1], claims that the Rose-Cross order showed itself publicly every one hundred and eight years and at each one of these public manifestations they proceeded to open a tomb that contained documents. This information is of much interest when considered in relation to the happenings at Rennes. In fact, it was in 1783 that Abbé Bigou drew up the epitaph that appeared on the Blanchefort tomb and concealed the documents within the church. Then exactly one hundred and eight years later in 1891, Bérenger Saunière found these documents and proceeded to open the Blanchefort tomb. Then if a further one hundred and eight years are added on to 1891, the date of 1999 is reached, the last year of the second thousand years of our era. This date is much favoured for speculations and prophetic claims by those who are believers in the theory of cycles. Without doubt, here we have a key that will explain the interest long taken in Rennes by esoteric sects and can account for the troubled atmosphere that they have succeeded in creating there.

The traveller will also smile at the naïvety of those searchers after treasure, who having met with little success, have invaded the church at Rennes. Attracted by the insistent strangeness of its stucco and plaster inhabitants, they have not realized that they should be concerned with

---

1. Jacques Duchaussoy. *Bacon, Shakespeare, Saint-Germain*, Paris, La Colombe, 1962. Note in particular pages 199–200 and 212–222.

rebus-puzzles like those we might find in some illustrated magazine, rather than with mechanical dolls by Vaucanson.

For them there is no doubt that these statues were hollow or fakes, or fitted with some kind of secret mechanism. They will probe here, lift up there and some of them would even tear out the eye of the devil, convinced that he is hiding a button which they think will open some door, or perhaps they would almost throw to the ground the emaciated satyr who supports the stoup. They do not know that the right tool for the searcher is neither the pick nor the mattock, but the brain. In addition, they do not possess that touch of spontaneity, which alone can spur our reasoning towards the broad fields of discovery.

ooOOoo

PART FOUR

DANGER THREATENS

The visit to the Palace of Visions is ended. We can now hope to get back once more to that familiar reality which characterises a calendar, a newspaper, a radio or television set; that of facts which can be verified, that of reports, and sometimes of different viewpoints. But here in the lost corners of the Razès, do not let us be too sure that this reality is sufficient to disperse the mirage and reassure us.

Guillaume Servin, agent of the regal powers, who was assassinated in 1340 by the noble counterfeiters of Bézu, is not the only person to meet a violent death because he became too interested in the gold of Rennes.

On 27th May 1732, the Curé of Niort-de-Saux, Bernard Mongé, was discovered at daybreak stretched out before the gateway to his garden, dead, with his skull smashed.

His assassin, named François de Montroux, was none other than the tutor to Marie de Négri d'Ables, the wife-to-be of François d'Hautpoul, Marquis of Blanchefort. Shortly after the crime, Montroux, who was bailiff of the district of Sault, left the area and so was unable to be present as witness at the wedding of his pupil. The motive for this murder, at least so it would appear, was pointless. Montroux had sought to advance his would-be claims on the presbytery of Niort-de-Saux, which Mongé would not agree to concede. After a period of banishment, Montroux returned to the district. As to the presbytery in dispute, it was purchased by François d'Hautpoul de Blanchefort with money lent to him by his wife's former tutor.

On the morning of All Saints Day in 1897, Abbé Antoine Gélis, Curé of Coustaussa, opposite Rennes, was found dead in his Presbytery. This is how the local newspaper, the *Aude Courier* (then published under the motto borrowed from the Saluki Law, "Christ loves the Francs") reported the story:

> Lying in a pool of blood with which his priestly robe was deeply stained, the victim had his arms and hands wrapped tightly around one knee that was drawn up to his chest. Abbé Gélis, whom his murderer had struck with violence and unheard of relentlessness, bore not less than twelve to fourteen horrendous wounds upon his head, a little above the nape of his neck. The skull was fractured in many places, so that the brain was exposed. Three wounds of lesser severity even showed on the face of the corpse.

Extensive bloodstains spattered the walls and ceiling of the kitchen. While some of the wounds seem to have been inflicted with the aid of a blunt instrument, certain others seem to have been caused by a cutting tool. The victim, to all appearances, did not succumb without offering desperate resistance. Money, amounting to one thousand five hundred francs, was found intact, though the drawers were open and the murderer had rummaged through all the furniture. Why was this? If it was not the intent to steal money, shares, or any other valuables, had the assassin, who had hunted everywhere so minutely, perhaps caused a document to disappear? This seems a simple explanation. However, some years ago, masked men did break into the presbytery, though it was never discovered who were responsible for the incident. The most profound mystery surrounds this horrible tragedy. No witness, no suspicions, no clues to follow. God alone knows the culprit.

This newspaper was not mistaken; the crime was never solved. At Abbé Gélis' funeral there was a large crowd. At the ceremony one could not fail to notice the presence of two colleagues, the Curés of Rennes-les-Bains and Rennes-le-Château, namely Abbés Boudet and Saunière.

Today, this affair is so thrust back into subconscious memories, including those of the three punctilious archivists of the diocese of Carcassonne, that we should never have known of it except by chance. In 1963 we met an aged but extremely learned Priest, Abbé Joseph

Courtauly, the Curé of Villarzel du Razès. With his advancing years, this Priest had become very wary and went so far as to refuse to open his door to the Vicar-General of the diocese. Here, as we recorded them on magnetic tape, are the fascinating confidences that he shared with us.

In 1908, I spent two months with Saunière at Rennes-le-Château; I was then barely eighteen years old. The village was admirably situated, but very windy. Saunière was a remarkable man. With his assistance I was able to produce a small painting in the Rennes church: he insisted upon the smallest details.

...There was Boudet, of course. He signed himself Edmond Boudet, though his name was really Jean-Jacques-Henri Boudet. It was quite a business, the Boudet affair. He left Rennes-les-Bains in May 1914 having had trouble with the diocesan authorities. His manuscripts had been destroyed in his presence, his book *Lazare* having been burnt. The diocesan missionary Abbé Rescanière then became Curé of Rennes-les-Bains in May 1914. He tried to throw light upon the Boudet–Saunière business, but about one or two o'clock in the morning one Monday — it was 1st February 1915 — he must have received two visitors who could never be traced.

That morning he was found dead, fully dressed and lying on the floor. The reason for his death is still a mystery[1]. Boudet, now very depressed, was living at Axat. He had decided to write to the diocese on the

---

1. Some time before his death Abbé Rescanière had been the victim of an attack, in which he suffered a knife wound. (Author's note).

26th March 1915 on the very subject of Rescanière, but when the Bishop's delegate arrived onThursday, 30th March 1915, about eight o'clock in the evening, Abbé Boudet had already died in dreadful agony a little while earlier. In the course of that day he had received a visit from two men…

There were other strange deaths about that time, such as that of the Curé of Coustaussa. He had gone to look for coins at Rennes-les-Bains. He was assassinated by stab wounds from a dagger. Neither the assassin nor the weapon was ever discovered.

…The tombstones at Rennes-le-Château were copied by Stublein, but his book was destroyed, though it is not known exactly why. I am probably the only person to have this book. It was during Abbé Mocquin's time…

It was at this point of the conversation that the aged Abbé Courtauly had a sensational surprise for us, which at the same time gave to us the most reliable verification.

"M. l'Abbé," we enquired, "has the treasure of Rennes ever really existed?"

His reply was,

"It is a real treasure we have here. Besides, I have preserved Saunière's coins which you now see displayed before you."

The old man then took out of two caskets, a superb collection of coins, saying to us,

See, we are not talking about the Saint-Louis era here. These are much earlier. They are certainly not coins of that period, but are dated between A.D. 600 and 700. They are coins of Dagobert. There are even some from the time of the Visigoths. What I possess here are two collections of this period. They bear the stamp of the Merovingians.

Without doubt we were the last ones to have discussed the enigma of Rennes with the old Abbé Courtauly. He died during the following year, in November 1964[1].

Bérenger Saunière's death on 22nd January in no respect extinguished the interest shown by some people in this mysterious affair. In fact, since that time the diocesan authorities at Carcassonne had never ceased to follow closely all that had occurred at Rennes-le-Château. It was particularly concerned with finding out, either directly or through intermediate sources, exactly what was the relationship that Bérenger had maintained with his servant, Marie Denarnaud. But she revealed nothing that could satisfy these enquiries. The hope remained that with advancing age she would at last give way.

In 1945 Marie Denarnaud had reached the age of seventy-seven years. Now at that time, it happened that one of her distant relations was in a difficult position once the Liberation had taken place. The patriotism of this relative during the years of occupation had not been completely established and he had been interned in a camp in the

---

1. In its obituary notice, the *Religious Weekly of the Diocese of Carcassonne* of 17th December, states regarding Abbé Courtauly; "His friends were somewhat envious of the contents of his library", and also, "It was not in every case that his trails met with success."

neighbourhood. The diocesan authorities then conceived the idea of a deal. The management of this plan was given over to a Priest, distinguished during the Resistance, whom the electors had just sent up to the Assembly. If the prisoner undertook to persuade his relative to give up her property at Rennes-le-Château he would soon be granted his freedom. The offender certainly did not refuse this pardon. But if the clerical parliamentarian had given his word, he was the only one who kept it.

The change in the bank notes, which was unexpectedly ordered by the Ramadier government, ruined the aged servant. Up to this time, for the past thirty years she had been living free from any anxiety. On the day when the order came into effect, she burned in her garden enormous bundles of bank-notes that had suddenly become unusable.

Shortly afterwards, it was to an hotelier, M. Noël Corbu, that Marie Denarnaud granted a lease for life on Bérenger Saunière's property. Having the best of intentions, the new owner decided to keep the old lady there and to look after her. No sooner had he moved in, than he learned by chance that there was buried treasure nearby. We can enjoy picturing his surprise at this sudden revelation. In any case, he did not doubt it for one moment: like the old labourer's children in La Fontaine's fable, he worked conscientiously and hard. How could he have failed to be encouraged by this circumstance?

Marie certainly stayed as silent as the effaced tombs in the cemetery, but she had agreed to pass over to M. Corbu the few remaining papers she held, which had belonged to her former master. However, one day she did venture a half-confidence:

"Before I die," said she to the hotelier, who has personally recounted the story, "I will tell you a secret that will make you a man of power." However, on the 29th January 1953 Marie Denarnaud was seized by a stroke.

"I was at her bedside," relates M. Noël Corbu. "She took me by the hand, looked into my eyes, and in a final burst of energy she attempted to keep her promise and to talk to me. Her blanched lips quivered urgently. She spoke for a long time but no intelligible sounds could emerge from her paralysed throat."

On the following day at the age of eighty-five years, Marie Denarnaud passed away and was buried beside Bérenger Saunière, still guarding the secret that she alone had shared with him.

M. René Descadeillas, keeper of the library at Carcassonne, an erudite and well-informed man, was an expert on the history of the ancient capital of the Razès. To this subject he has dedicated the important work that, during the course of our investigations, we have had reason to quote on several occasions. In 1966 we went to pay him a visit and his words to us were,

Bérenger Saunière was nothing but a common swindler, who enjoyed mystifying people. He was artful, but uncultured, almost ignorant. As to the origin of his fortune, there is no mystery about that. It was passed over to him in the form of gifts by rich folk who preserved their anonymity to avoid upsetting their heirs. In addition, he took part in the traffic in Masses. The manuscripts? He never found any. He put them together himself in order to impress his dupes. As to the decoration of his church, he bought it all ready-made in Paris, from near Saint-Sulpice.

This outburst quite considerably diminished the convincing effect of our investigations that had led us thus far. In fact we would have felt quite justified in quitting the church of Rennes-le-Château. But the doubt that troubled us was due to change to downright puzzlement when we learned some time later that the erudite archivist, along with certain of his friends, had himself undertaken a series of excavations at Rennes-le-Château.

On Saturday 31st March 1956, M. Descadeillas, M. Malacan, a doctor of great erudition, M. Brunon, an optician and M. Despeyronat, whose besotting passion is radiesthesia, busied themselves at Rennes-le-Château. At first they excavated inside the church, in front of the high altar, where once lay the "Chevalier's Stone" under which Bérenger Saunière had found a small hoard within an earthenware pot. In this location the searchers now found a human skull bearing a gash on its crown. Thanks to the kindness of Doctor Malacan, who has preserved it, we have been able to examine and photograph this skull. It is that of a man, and the gash that it displays is regular in shape and without splinters. It would appear to be a ritual wound, analogous to those on skulls that have been dug up in the Merovingian cemeteries of Lorraine and of Montferrand in the Aude[1] or on the head of the anthropomorphic menhir at Rennes-les-Bains, which is known by the name of Saint Dagobert. The searchers then went to Bérenger Saunière's garden and proceeded to dig a hole. At a depth of about one and a half metres they came to the conclusion that someone had been there before them. This belief then took a form that was far from reassuring. In fact, they saw appearing under the blades of their pickaxes, three corpses in a state of decomposition; scraps of flesh, hair and moustaches still adhered to the bones. On the bodies were knitted fabrics and fragments of clothing. The corpses comprised three men about thirty-five years old. They had been struck by several bullets. A police captain and an official doctor then came to inspect the corpses. The inquest was entrusted to an examining magistrate, but came to no conclusion. No one ever identified the victims, no one ever discovered their assassins.

In 1960 an official from Paris arrived in his turn at Rennes-le-Château. He announced that he held a permit duly signed and in good order, which he had just had approved by the diocese of Carcassonne, with the object of opening new excavations, this time inside the church. In order to do this he sought and soon obtained the authorisation of the municipality. However, they may have been subjected to a little persuasion. It was nevertheless

---

1. A Carolingian cartulary points out that the skulls of the dead were ritually pierced in order to prevent their return. Followers of geomancy also made use of pierced skulls in the search for treasure.

agreed by all parties that the work should not be made public. Helped by three friends, the official started his investigations. On each occasion, in order to avoid unwelcome visitors, the whole party locked themselves within the church.

One evening in the spring of 1960, when he opened the door of the building to leave, the researcher from Paris saw a dark mass crashing down upon him. He hardly had enough time to spring back to safety.

"What saved me," he repeated later," was the sun, which at that moment was setting. I could therefore see in a flash the shadow of the falling object so was just able to avoid it."

A baulk of timber had been placed against the door, in such a way as to crash down as the door was opened. The survivor decided that he had experienced quite enough. He left the district and never came back.

On 20th May 1968, Noël Corbu, the last owner of the property and papers of Bérenger Saunière, met a violent death in a road accident between Castelnaudary and Carcassonne. Did this accident resemble that which occurred on 20th February 1967 and cost the life of someone else who was curious about the mysteries of Rennes, namely Fakhar Ul Islam who was found on the railway track near Melun, having fallen from the Paris–Geneva express? The fact remains that M. Corbu was dragged, unrecognisable, from the shapeless debris of his Renault 16.

Some days later on 18th June 1968, Mgr. Boyer, Vicar General of the diocese of Carcassonne, whose interest brought him so close to the enigma, just escaped a similar fate. Near Carcassonne, at the place known as Devils Bridge, his car was crushed against a post. With his leg broken, his ribs fractured, and a wound on his head, the prelate only escaped by a miracle.

Abbé Maurice-René Mazières, Curé of Villesèquelande, situated near Carcassonne, is the most loveable and the most level-headed of men. His eyes are black and frank, his countenance massive but softened by his head of whitened hair. This old lawyer who took his orders late in life, is one of the best historians of the Razès, and one of the most erudite correspondents of the learned Society of Arts and Sciences of Carcassonne. How could he not become passionately fond of the mysteries of Rennes, since he knows every stone in the place?

One evening we went to knock at his door without giving him any warning. He opened it wide to us, after having made sure through the spy-hole that we did not have too evil an appearance. In his presbytery, which was as austere and bare as a monk's cell, we spoke for an entire evening about the singular story that we have just recounted to you. He revealed to us in full many aspects, so as to guide our enquiries.

"In short," said Abbé Mazières to us, at the end of a lengthy discussion, "is it your intention to study the records sufficiently to enable you to write a complete book on this business?"

"That is exactly my intention."

After refilling our glasses for a last time with an unforgettable Armagnac, Abbé Mazières looked me straight in the eye and said quietly,

"I understand that you have become very interested in this affair; it also fascinates me. But it is necessary that I should forewarn you: this will involve a certain element of danger…"

ooOOoo

INDEX OF PRINCIPAL PERSONS

BEAUSÉJOUR (Paul-Félix Beurain de). — Bishop of Carcassonne from 1902 to 1930.

BIEIL (Jean-François-Victor). — Born 19th February 1835 at Boulogne-sur-Gesse (Haute-Garonne), ordained as Priest 1858, Director of the seminary of Saint-Sulpice in 1875, Vicar General of the Diocese of Paris. Died 23rd January 1898 at Salies-du-Salat (Haute-Garonne).

BIGOU (Antoine). — Born 18th April 1719 at Sournia. Curé of Rennes-le-Château from 1774 to 1790. Took the oath for the office of Priest with restriction 20th February1791, but this was not accepted. Died 21st March 1794 at Sabadell (Spain).

BIGOU (Jean). — Born 1702. Curé of Rennes-le-Château from 1736 to 1774. Died in 1776 at Rennes-le-Château.

BILLARD (Félix-Arsène). — Bishop of Carcassonne from 1881 to 1902.

BOUDET (Jean-Jacques-Henri). — Born at Quillan (Aude) 16th November 1837. Ordained as Priest 25th December 1861. Curé of Rennes-les-Bains from 1872 to 1914. Died 30th March 1915 at Axat (Aude).

CALVÉ (Emma). — Born 15th August 1858 at Decazeville
(Aveyron). Died 6th January 1942 at Millau (Aveyron).

CAYRON (Émile-François-Henri-Géraude de). — Born
11th December 1807 at Aubin (Aveyron). Ordained as
Priest in 1833. Curé of Saint-Laurent-de-Cabrerisse
(Aude). Died 3rd January 1897 at Toulouse (Haute-
Garonne).

COURTAULY (Guillaume-Jean-Joseph). — Born 31st
May 1890 at Villarzel-du-Razès (Aude). Ordained as
Priest in 1921. Died 11th November 1964 at Villarzel-
du-Razès (Aude).

DENARNAUD (Marie). — Born in 1868 at Esperaza
(Aude). Died 29th January 1953 at Rennes-le-
Château (Aude).

GÉLIS (Jean-Antoine-Maurice). — Born 1st April 1827
at Villesèquelande (Aude). Curé of Coustaussa (Aude)
in 1857. Died 1st November 1897 at Coustaussa (Aude).

HABSBOURG (Jean-Stéphane de, Comte de Méran, Baron
de Brandhof). — Born in 1867. Married in 1891 to
Ladislaja de Lamberg. Died in 1947.

HOFFET (Émile-Henri). — Born 11th May 1873 at
Schitigheim. Died 3rd March 1946 at Paris.

MOCQUIN (Charles-Eugène). — Curé of Rennes-le-Château (Aude) from 1881 to 1884.

RESCANIÈRES (Joseph-Marie-Casimir). — Curé of Rennes-les-Bains (Aude) from 1914 to 1915.

SAUNIÈRE (François-Bérenger). — Born 11th April 1852 at Montazels (Aude). Ordained as Priest in 1879. Curé of Rennes-le-Château (Aude) 1st June 1885. Interdicted 11th April 1915. Died 22nd January 1917 at Rennes-le-Château (Aude).

ooOOoo

BIBLIOGRAPHY

ABADAL — *Del reino de Tolosa al reino de Toledo* Madrid, 1960.

ARNOLD (Paul). — *Histoire des Rose-Croix.* Paris, 1955.

BLANCASALL (Madeleine). — *Les descendants mérovingiens ou l'énigme du Razès wisigoth.* (translated from the German by Walter Celse-Nazaire). Geneva.

BOUDET (H.). — *La vraie langue Celtique et le cromleck de Rennes-les-Bains,* Carcassonne. 1886.
Lazare Veni foras, 1891.
Bulletin de la Société des études scientifiques de l'Aude. Carcassonne.
Buts de promenade et objets curieux des environs de Rennes-les-Bains. Toulouse, s.d.(undated).

DESCADEILLAS (René). — *Rennes et ses derniers seigneurs.* Toulouse, 1964.
Notice sur Rennes-le-Château et l'abbé Saunière. Carcassonne, 1962.

FÉDIÉ (Louis). — *Histoire du comté de Razès et du diocèse d'Alet.* Carcassonne, 1880.

FEUGÈRE (Pierre). — *Le Serpent Rouge.*

JAFFUS (A.). — *La cité de Carcassonne et les trésors des Wisigoths.* Carcassonne, s.d.(undated).

JAFFUS (F.). — *La cité de Carcassonne a-t-elle renfermé une partie des trésors du temple de Jérusalem?* Carcassonne, 1867.

LABOUISSE-ROCHEFORT. — *Voyage à Rennes-les-Bains.* Paris, 1832.

LAROQUE — *Annuaire historique et généalogique de la province de Languedoc.* Paris, 1861.

LASSERRE (Joseph-Théodore). — *Recherches historiques sur la ville d'Alet et son ancien diocèse.* Carcassonne, 1877.
Histoire du pèlerinage de Notre-Dame-de-Marceille, près Limoux. 1891.

LIZOP (R.). — *Un peuple gaulois inconnu dans la haute vallée de l'Aude.* In *Annales du Midi*, *Vol. 69.* April 1957.

LOBINEAU (Henri). — *Généalogie des rois mérovingiens et origine des diverses familles françaises et étrangères de souche mérovingienne.* After Abbé Pichon, Dr. Hervé and The

Parchments of Abbé Saunière, Curé of Rennes-le-Château. Geneva, 1956.

Dossiers Secrets. Paris 17, Quai de Montebello.

MAZIÈRES (Maurice-René). — La venue et le séjour des Templiers du Roussillon à la fin du XIIIᵉ siècle et au début du XIVᵉ siècle dans la vallée du Bézu (Aude). In Mémoires de la Société des Arts et Sciences de Carcassonne. 4ᵗʰ Series,Vol. III. 1957-1959.

MÉTRAUX (Maurice). — Les "Blanquefort" et les origines vikings dites normandes de la Guyenne sous la féodalité. Bordeaux, 1963.

ROUX (S.). — L'affaire de Rennes-le-Château. Levallois-Perret, s.d.(undated).

STUBLEIN (Eugène). — Pierres gravées du Languedoc. Limoux, 1884. (Taken in part from plates XVI to XXIII, edited by Abbé Joseph Courtauly, Villarzel-du-Razès. 1962).

Rennes-les-Bains: description, s.l.n.d.(undated).

VAISÈTTE (Dom) and VIC (Dom de). — Histoire générale du Languedoc.

VIDAL (J.-M.). — Note sur la parenté de Benoit XII. s.l.n.d.(undated).

SOURCE MANUSCRIPTS:

National Archives. — Ms. JJ 68 No. 348.

Archives of The Department of The Aude. — Series 0: Rennes-le-Château.

Private Archives of M.R. Chésa.

MAZIÈRES (M.-R.). — *Notes manuscrites sur l'histoire du Razès.* (Supplied by their Author).

SAUNIÈRE (François Bérenger.). — *A manuscript exercise book.* (from the private archives of M. Noël Corbu).

ooOOoo